A Van of One's Own

Biddy Wells grew up in south Wales and has been a writer all her life. She has a long-standing interest in folk music and has written scores of songs, many of which have been recorded in various musical ensembles. A decade ago she began writing prose, describing the life she saw around her through her particular lens. Her journey to Portugal marked the first time that her journal became a close and essential companion. She has a son and a daughter and currently lives in mid Wales with her partner. *A Van of One's Own* is her first book.

A Van of One's Own

Biddy Wells

Parthian, Cardigan SA43 1ED
www.parthianbooks.com
First published in 2017
© Biddy Wells
ISBN 9781910901991
Cover design Syncopated Pandemonium
Cover by Biddy Wells
Interior illustrations by Seren Stacey
Typeset by Elaine Sharples
Printed by Pulsio Sarl
Published with the financial support of the Welsh Books Council
British Library Cataloguing in Publication Data
A cataloguing record for this book is available from the British Library.

Part One

This is one of those perfect moments. The morning is fresh, but not cold. The sun, now low, will rise up and shine all day in a bright blue sky, untroubled by clouds. There are a few clouds at this early hour, but they are small and round and are already dispersing into invisibility. Nothing dark and glowering, no aeroplane trails. I have moved my chair into the sun. It's going to be a hot day.

I am on the west coast of France, at a slightly overpriced campsite. There's no one else around, though just one month ago tents, caravans and campervans would have been crammed cheek by jowl into this small area of grass plots, each one forty or so square metres and hemmed in with high hedges. It is old school French camping and I love it. I also love the fact that almost every town and village has a campsite like this. You rent your little plot and do what you like. Mostly that means you make a home of your holiday abode, putting out tables and chairs, a washing line, perhaps a barbecue. I prefer France out of season, and September seems to have the best weather/peacefulness balance. The weather this August was terrible, according to locals. I have come to think of August as the February of the summer: often an unsettling turning point between seasons. But if September has got its act together and settles into mellowness, it can be a golden month. The stirred-up Atlantic becomes calmer and clearer, the wind drops, and everything relaxes. Most outdoor pools have been drained, ready for the coming winter, though the pool here is still operational and, apparently, heated. That is what I am paying for, and I feel obliged to use it and get my money's worth even though, in all honesty, it's cold.

I have just made a pot of tea. My teapot is the opposite of a Tardis – smaller than it looks – and it's cracked. I didn't mind at first, but over time the crack has become a dark, threatening scar. I keep the pot mostly for sentimental reasons and because it makes a good cup of tea. There might well come a time when I will no longer need to comment critically on every little thing, cracks in teapots or nasty clouds, but I am not there yet. A continuous stream of judgements compete for space in my brain. The first thought I had this morning was: 'My life didn't really have room for me in it.' I wanted to write that down quickly, before I forgot it. My second thought was: 'Must get the kettle on.' My third, which was almost simultaneous, was: 'It's such a long way to the loos, and I have to go right now.' In what order was I to achieve these vital tasks? Skip to the end: loos, kettle, write down thought. It was a high-risk strategy, but it worked.

Ideas usually come to me when I am walking, driving or nearly asleep. I have had brilliant opening lines just appear in my mind, starting points that I thought would surely lead to writings worth reading (if only I'd had a pen!). Some seemed so good that I thought I could not possibly fail to remember them. I believed that I would store these treasures in my memory until some magic time when I would be less busy – a time of freedom, solitude and peace. I was hanging on for this pause in routine – an escape from the closed circles in my life. Life had become little more than a series of endlessly repeating cycles, or that's how it had begun to feel. There was nothing wrong with any of its parts, but altogether it was making me weary. 'Ennui' describes the state I was in: dissatisfaction, tedium, lack of excitement. That sounds pretty accurate.

I read the line that, sensibly, I have written down: 'My life did not have room for me in it.' No room for *me,* even though I have come to feel so small: like the reverse-Tardis teapot, not as big as I might appear. A feeling had been welling up inside me: an overwhelming desire to stretch my wings and expand somehow. I had to take the plunge, not wait for some fantasy future opportunity to come along. What was I waiting for, retirement?

I can see how good my life was – how extremely fortunate I was to live in a beautiful part of an untroubled and relatively peaceful country. I had good work, money coming in and all the things that make for a liveable life – a life much easier than so many that have been ruined by the way the world is.

I am truly grateful that I was born into this relative privilege, but being merely grateful is not enough. I'm not fulfilling my potential. I could assert that, at least, I am not living in a war zone, or starving, or homeless. But 'at least' seems a flimsy, half-hearted way to live life.

I think about people who have achieved great feats in the world of art, science, medicine and so on. But I am not one of them. I have made no mark, invented nothing. I am comfortable being ordinary, but uncomfortable with the place in which I find myself. I am unfulfilled – not fully present. I am waiting for something, marking time.

I am grateful for my life, but perhaps real gratitude would mean using my privilege to go beyond merely struggling and getting through the day. Perhaps real gratitude would mean recognising, without guilt, my good fortune and running with it: celebrating it and using it to do something not half-hearted. I wonder what I can do with my good fortune.

Today, though, I feel blessed. Here I am in the sunshine, free of the routines of my newly old life. I have the time and space to write, for the first time in years. The pen looping its way across the paper somehow untangles the twisted spaghetti in my head, and that feels very good. If it seems bit self-indulgent, I don't care. The noisy road-sweeping lorry passes for the third time this morning. I don't mind it; every time I go to France, there is always some machine disturbing the early part of the morning – life going on. It has nothing to do with me. I hear birds twittering in the small trees all around the site. Peace is relative. It's all good.

I am basking in a feeling of accomplishment. I saved up for this trip, prepared for it and found the courage to follow my heart, which meant working through some thoughts that tried pretty hard to prevent me from doing it. All that fear! 'What am I doing giving up my home, security and income for a journey into the unknown? What will I have to come back to? Where will I belong?' All this before I had made a single step on the road. And the answer is always the same: 'I don't know.' But *why* am I doing it? That is easier to answer: I just have to be free.

The sun is up above the treetops now. Something inside me has softened just a tad – melted, opened up. Maybe there could be a little bit of room for me. My sleepy-headed daughter emerges from her tent into the increasing heat. We drink tea in delicious silence.

*

For reasons I didn't understand, I just knew I had to go to Portugal. This knowing had started many months earlier: a deep longing, which crept in during the night. I would wake up feeling that I just had to go there, to that unfamiliar place. I assumed this meant I would take a holiday with my partner, David. Previously, we had explored France together in his camper, which had been fun. Quietly, though, inside my mind, the notion grew into something much bigger than a holiday. We vaguely discussed making this trip together, but as things evolved over the spring it became clear that nobody was coming with me. If I wanted to go, I would have to go alone. Portugal is not all that far away, or exotic, or dangerous, but it felt like a huge stretch for me to leave my partner, family, job and home and just go off. An overland solo trip lasting months in an ancient little campervan was not the kind of thing I did. But it was something I was about to do.

The summer seemed to go on too long as I prepared to leave my old life. I had commitments until September, and while I tied up various loose ends people would ask the same handful of questions: 'Where will you stay? How long are you going for? What will you do? When will you be back? Are you scared? Why Portugal?' I didn't know. Actually, I was scared. Fear gnawed at me a lot of the time as I prepared to leave, but it didn't overwhelm my desire to go. I had decided to face my fear anyway. There was no question of my not going.

One afternoon, my daughter phoned to say she had some leave from work and could come with me for the first few days of my trip, if I'd like.

'But maybe that'll take something away, Mum; maybe you need to do all of it alone?' she asked. I thought it over really carefully for about five seconds.

'No, it would be really wonderful for us to have some time together. It's a precious opportunity,' I told her. What a blessing it was that my daughter and I could share this small part of my big adventure. I had no return ticket, no re-entry protocol and no plans about coming back.

The twenty-year-old van I'd bought two weeks before the start of my trip was fairly small and quite rusty, but seemed to be mechanically sound. Most importantly, it was cheap, thus making the trip a possibility rather than a fantasy. It spent a week in the garage being serviced and prepared for all that might happen on the road, and another week being equipped with a solar panel, lighting and 12v power. It had already been converted into a camper with a basic kitchen and a very comfortable sofa bed. We set off from Wales one warm September morning, my daughter and me. I learned to drive the van as we headed for the ferry to France. We also had a brand new GPS that my brother had given me for my birthday – it arrived the day before we left. My daughter named it Tanya, as she thought its female voice sounded a bit Tanya-like. I had just decided upon Myfanwy for the van, and so it became a girlie sort of road trip. All went well: we sailed to Roscoff and on our route from Brittany to Bordeaux, where my daughter and I said goodbye, we stayed at some lovely little camp sites, enjoying beachlife and lovely lunches. I couldn't have asked for a more auspicious beginning to my journey.

Swinging by the airport had looked very simple when I was back home browsing the map, even for a wimp like me who doesn't do airports, let alone in an unfamiliar country whilst driving a long wheelbase van on the wrong side of the road and all. I knew nothing about terminals and parking and limited height barriers. Now I do, and it's quite straightforward, of course; but leaving the airport, I wove through hot Saturday traffic with a lump in my throat and a rising feeling of anxiety.

What did I think I was doing? I was alone in a strange place, with no real plan except to get to Portugal within a few weeks. It suddenly felt pointless and overwhelming. I pulled myself together and headed for the nearest small town. I planned to sit in a gorgeous cafe and, over a large cafe-au-lait and almond croissants, or maybe a beautifully retro croque monsieur, I would plot a scenic route to a picturesque place where I would spend the evening and night. When I found the *centre-ville*, I realised that I was not in the mood to enjoy sitting alone in a cafe; I was too heavy of heart. Feeling despondent, I pushed on, giving up the idea of comforting food.

*

I have a very useful book: a sort of bible for campervanners. It gives the coordinates and specifications for thousands of *aires de camping-car*, which are official parkups – often free – where campervanners can get water, empty their waste and stay safely for a night or more. Caravans and tents are not admitted. The book shows colour photos of each *aire*. At first glance one is confronted by hundreds of pictures of parking bays; some are utilitarian, concrete lots, but others are situated in rural, leafy glades. Sometimes their waste and water facilities are also featured. Photographs of drive-over drains and sewage disposal points are not pretty, and it's a strangely ugly book, yet over time it becomes vital and comforting. I would not travel in a campervan without it now. Arriving at an *aire,* I usually feel safe and welcome, wherever I am. France is particularly campervan friendly, boasting *aires* in most villages, towns, cities and beauty spots. Spain and Portugal are gradually beginning to follow suit.

*

After a while, I arrived at an *aire* that was highly recommended in my book – and I could see why. It overlooked an enormous beautiful lake and occupied a very spacious, sandy compound, with plenty of shade from mature trees. Very aware of being alone, I felt awkward, not carefree like I had been only the day before. I had to take a ticket and pay on entry, but I didn't understand the system and got muddled. Feeling stupid, I had to ask for help. It was difficult to find the right spot where my solar panel could gain as much sun as possible, so I drove round and round until I settled on a spot, then rejected it, reparked and got overheated and flustered. I had no one to laugh with and felt isolated and sad.

I had a quick, slightly self-conscious swim in the lake, which was cooling and soothing. Returning to the van, I realised I had mislaid my phone. I searched everywhere, revisited the ticket barrier, panicked and searched the van again, but had no luck. I sat quietly and thought through my plan B for communication. I had brought my old phone with me for just such a situation, but I had no idea where I had hidden it, and I felt it was a bit soon to have suffered such a calamity – out of contact on the same day I had waved off my lovely daughter, who had been such excellent company and a wonderful copilot! The lump in my throat returned and grew until I had to let it go. I sat and cried, then flopped down on the sofa bed and lay there for a while, feeling a bit sorry for myself. My hand slipped over the edge of the upholstery, down the side and – there was my phone, wedged against the cupboard! I cried some more, kissed my phone and laughed. I didn't know what I was doing; it all seemed so ridiculous, laughable. I ate a picnic supper of bread and cheese, drank a couple of glasses of wine and had an early night. I woke at three, wishing it was already dawn so I could make tea and a fresh start. Three in the morning is a fretful, menacing, awful time, and, to top it off, I was covered in itching bites. Things had to get better.

*

Several years ago, I took to my bed and stayed there, alone, for a long, long time, only leaving it when something seemed to be worth the immense effort of getting up – which was seldom. Some days I would walk a neighbour's dog, and I guess I must have shopped occasionally, though I had little interest in food. It's a blur, that time. I lost a lot of weight and remember seeing myself in the mirror, noting that I had the slimness of figure – that emaciated look – for which some women strive. Yet it didn't matter one iota to me what I looked like; I was simply wasting away from a lack of self-care. I was depressed – truly unwell, not just a bit fed up. It hadn't been a conscious choice to slip out of the flow of life; it was something beyond my control. If I allow myself to enter the memory of that time, I can catch glimpses of the way I felt. It was excruciating. I felt as if I was in the process of dying an extremely slow death. I was fighting an invisible force that was hellbent on crushing me. I had no means of rising up against it, and, eventually, I surrendered and accepted my new reality. The invisible force won.

After a great deal of rest and isolation from the pressures of life outside my bedroom, something shifted and the malaise began to subside. Thanks to my mother's telephone support and some amazingly caring friends, who regularly invited me to eat with them even though I was probably not great company, I got stronger and started to look after myself. I got back on my feet, but after so long out of rhythm with the rest of the world, it was hard to get into step. In fact, I realised I would never catch up; I'd never be the same again or get back to where I had been before I fell apart. And where was that? It hadn't been such a wonderful place, if I was honest, and anyway, it was lost to me then – gone forever.

And now, years later, I had taken to the road – alone. I am not adventurous. I didn't want to go anywhere that involved vaccinations or flying. I am cautious by nature: a fearful rabbit who worries about things that might never happen. Portugal was close enough that I could imagine going there and getting there; plus, I had friends who happened to be staying in the Algarve and would welcome me. But it was also far away enough that I could leave everything behind me at a safe distance. What I was hoping to achieve by this flight from my life was not clear to me. I can see that taking to my bed and taking to the road seem somehow related to each other: each is an escape from normal life. Was this roadtrip all about evasion? And if it was, would it provide only a temporary shelter?

*

I have always been fascinated by maps – in fact, I get a little obsessed by them, feeling that as my eyes move over their lines and contours I am somehow preparing to travel their real-life counterparts. The world is so big, and I have only ever visited tiny areas not very far from home. Planning my trip, I would measure the distance from home to the ferry port, then plot how many journeys of this distance would get me to Portugal, then get distracted noticing how many times the British Isles fit into Africa, Russia, America, and so on. It was awesome. It *is* awesome. I live in a dot in a tiny country in a huge world. Looking at all those places I will never visit, I feel parochial, unworldly, untravelled.

The GPS my brother had bought me would be an invaluable tool for a single-handed journey, but the idea of following blindly the instructions of a gadget sounded unattractive to a map lover like me. I want to see the overview, get my bearings and create a mental picture before I set off. I have always relied on 'nat sav' (natural savvy), and it's hard to let go of that and trust a voice coming from a tiny box on the dashboard. Some time after Bordeaux, though, I realised I could rely on Tanya to guide me; she stays cool and unruffled, and I am starting to respect her. Sometimes I get quite angry with her, though: for example, when she takes me on twenty kilometres of very narrow track through a deserted pine forest in Landes. Once, she took me on a shortcut over a tiny bridge that was so acutely humpbacked I would still be teetering upon its pointed brow, had I not stopped abruptly and reversed onto the main road (there was nothing coming). We had words then, and I realised, afterwards, that I need to be more assertive, more involved. It's not enough to hand over all decisions to her. She is very literal about taking the shortest possible route, but I need to take roads that look wide enough for a van. She won't be offended; she'll just calmly reconfigure, and we'll get there in the end.

Travelling with Tanya means that I can employ the Completion Backward Principle, an idea I came across in the early eighties thanks to an album of that name by The Tubes.

The idea is that you visualise the end result you require (this can be anything), and you relax knowing that all the steps required to achieve it will appear effortlessly and in the correct order. It works brilliantly. Tanya is doing the same thing, using programmed information. Where does this information come from, I wonder? It's all a matter of trusting someone or something we don't necessarily understand, and I am starting to trust Tanya.

*

Continuing towards Spain, I decided to stop in Pays Basque, where, on the internet, I had found a little campsite that looked perfect. Tanya found the village and signs guided us to the entrance of the campsite, but I saw that it was closed. What was I going to do? I sat for a while, thinking, when a young woman called and waved from the driveway. '*Fermé*?' I gestured with a hand across my throat. '*Non, ouvert!*' she shouted, and opened the gate, much to my relief and joy. I had misread the sign, as I was getting tired and projecting the idea of failure onto current circumstances.

It was a truly tranquil spot: nobody else around. I cooked a casserole, drank some wonderful beers I bought from the tiny camp shop and began to feel relaxed. All night the rain hammered on the roof and came inside the back doors, but by morning it had stopped, and the day looked full of warm promise. Wasn't this how it used to be on all those camping holidays in Wales in the seventies? I seem to remember that it rained all night and every night, but a bright, dry morning always followed, during which the bedding could be dried out before the next shower drenched everything. Happy days.

There are few things I love more than to sleep close to the earth in a warm sleeping bag, under canvas, under rain. And here I was, revisiting wonderful camping memories in Myfanwy, complete with indoor kettle. Sadly, my three-way camping fridge was in a sorry state: warm and unpleasantly cheese-scented. I realised it no longer worked on gas.

I walk downhill to the village, passing sweet-faced goats and their kids. The church is simple and whitewashed, the houses pretty and typical Pays Basque: half-timbered under red pantile roofs, reminiscent of a Swiss alpine scene on a biscuit tin lid. Passing a few shops, I arrive at the wide river Adour, and walk along its bank for a while. The sky is soft and grey and, after so much rain, the water is high and full of mud and debris. Whole tree trunks float by silently, gradually overtaking me. The opposite bank seems a mile away, complete with a shabby château surrounded by a light mist.

After a second night at the little campsite I made an early start, and before long I crossed the border into Spain. For a few hours I seemed to be climbing up and up, weaving through industrial sprawl, surrounded by spectacular mountains reminiscent of the Pyrenées. I pushed on for as long as I could, anxious to find somewhere to spend the night.

The next stop was my first experience of a place that felt a bit dodgy. It was a campervan *aire* that was located on the banks of a river and sounded quite good on paper, but for some reason the planners had sited it in a nasty little alley at the abandoned edge of town. Any ideas I'd had about taking a refreshing evening dip were soon dispelled; this was not a place to undress and relax. I parked up next to the only other van and had a feeling that I needed to be on my guard. Sure enough; within minutes I was approached by a scruffily dressed man who reeked of booze and seemed pleased to have someone to talk to. I didn't share his enthusiasm, but I said hello. He stood at my door and got into his flow, proceeding to tell me, in French, all about the many problems that were being dealt him by life, the police and the mayor. After a while, I realised he was stuck on a repetitive loop, and I tried to ignore him, turning away and getting on with cooking, and he wandered off, much to my relief. Minutes later he returned, looking decidedly grumpy, and started the routine again. After four or five more visits, I got fed up and went for a less subtle approach, telling him to get lost. This seemed to do the trick.

As my French is almost passable, I was able follow what the problems-guy was ranting about. However, I have no grasp whatsoever of Spanish, and after he had gone, my Spanish neighbour took the opportunity to come over and welcome me to the dump. She was smiley and friendly and seemed concerned that I was alone. She talked enthusiastically for some time without pausing, adding a fair amount of body language, which helped a lot. I think she was saying things along the lines of, 'We must all stick together; this is a dodgy place and we must park very close, almost touching, to show that we are all together: a family. Come and have some coffee.' I nodded a great deal, unable to remember even how to say 'I don't understand.'

I was relieved when a couple more vans pulled in for the night and I was tightly flanked. It was beginning to grow dark and everyone had retreated to the sanctuary of their vans for the night. This is something that happens most evenings; the feeling of community quickly evaporates and, once again, we all become separate units isolated in our own little homes. It can be a bit of a relief, settling into one's own quiet space, but it can also feel a bit lonesome. Most people travel in couples, and so my aloneness, though I chose it, is highlighted at this point in the day. Still, I am getting quite comfortable with campervan life, and I felt relaxed now, gazing at the last remnants of light in the western sky.

Suddenly there was an unsmiling face at my window. The problems-guy had his nose pressed up against the glass, peering in. I snapped my curtains shut, locked the door and got ready for an early and possibly sleepless night.

Strangely, I slept like a log and felt elated to wake up safe and sound. I got some water from a lone tap, which was the only 'service facility' at the *aire*, then headed off in a southwesterly direction. The day became clearer and hotter, and I put a CD into the player to serenade me along the quiet roads through the mountains. I was heading for a destination and focussed on getting there as quickly as possible, though Myfanwy is more of a friendly old pony than a racehorse. I wasn't particularly enjoying the journey for its beauty or culture, but simply driving, sleeping, resting and eating. I was making progress and calculated that I could easily be in Algarve by the date on which I hoped to meet my friends from Wales.

In my bible of *aires,* I had spotted a parkup that was right next to a well-preserved castle in a small town of timber-framed buildings, just a short detour from the route I was travelling. I arrived mid-afternoon, when everything was, of course, shut. The streets were all lined with ancient wooden verandas, creating shady walkways beneath. There were plenty of houses, but only a few shops, and no people at all. It felt like a stage set: unreal, deserted. Perhaps everyone was having a nap; the heat was intense, and I fancied a siesta myself. With that in mind, I parked up next to the fabulous castle. I opened a window to let in the breeze and within seconds the van was full of flies – scores of them, a veritable plague. I realised the folly of travelling without mosquito nets and put up my one and only fly paper. Realising I couldn't stay in the van, infested and hot as a sauna, a moment longer, I closed the flies in and abandoned ship. I walked the silent, sweltering streets and viewed the church and the castle with its little stone hermitages. I wandered down to the mini supermarket, which was closed for the afternoon, and thought about my bare cupboards and infestation of flies. I sat with my bottle of water next to a fountain in the tiny village plaza, mercifully shaded by knobbly little trees. Three old men appeared and sat together on a bench, their comfortable silence suggesting lifelong friendship. We greeted each other with '¡Hola!' and sat in silence for a while. The church bell chimed five o'clock.

Finally the shop opened, and I bought an apple, bread, a tomato and some cheese. I returned to Myfanwy and counted well over a hundred flies stuck to the deadly sticky paper, and several more still buzzing about. I remembered that I had a plastic swatter that came with van. Within a short time I became expert at killing flies, sickening though it felt. It was me or them, and I won, but I could no longer open my windows. Thankfully, the night was cold up in the mountains, and I slept well again.

Next morning, with not a single living fly in the van, I hightailed it out of the *aire*, away from the dream-like town and along the long narrow lane that would connect me with the road to Salamanca. Within five minutes I had pulled over and was throwing up in a ditch. Was it the flies? Ah! I remembered now: the dodgy place with the single tap; the water had been a bit warm. How stupid of me! I had thought of lots of things in the planning stage, but not mozzie nets, and I had completely forgotten the warnings about suspicious taps.

Arriving at a campsite on the outskirts of Salamanca, I decide I have to get my fridge running on electricity and keep my meagre food supplies edible – not that I am eating much. I realise I don't have the right electric hook up adapter for Spain. The campsite receptionist directs me to a local shop that he says sells such things. I set off on my bicycle but I can't find the place, which I imagine from the description to be a camping shop on a nearby corner. I ask a few people, who point further and further away from the campsite, and I keep going. It's a challenge because I am sick and weak, but eventually I find the giant megastore on a huge intersection. Walking around the store is another big effort, but at least it's cooler than outside. I buy an adapter which I know is wrong, though the assistant insists it will work. It doesn't. It was a total waste of energy, pushing my exhausted body around for two hours; I still have no electricity. My fridge is now nothing more than a stinky cupboard. The next few days are a bit hazy: intense heat and a lot of showering, nil by mouth except bottled water. I am burning up, feverish, drenched in sweat and feeling lousy. I feel I ought to see the sights but I am too weak.

On Sunday I felt a bit stronger, so I got the bus into Salamanca centre. I walked under an arch and found myself in the city's main square, looking up at vast, almost golden sandstone edifices on every side. I felt lukewarm about it all, though, wandering about in my linen clothes – which I suddenly realised were scruffy and creased – surrounded by hundreds of very smartly dressed people, everyone in their Sunday best. I was trying to focus less on my attire and more on the architecture, but I was too exhausted and pathetic to appreciate its magnificence. I took a few photos to look at later, which is something I have always thought a bit ridiculous. I *must* be ill! I thought.

As people sat outside cafes enjoying food, company, sunshine and the view, I was walking across the Plaza Mayor where, just in front of me, a smart young woman strode purposefully. She was probably in her late twenties, my daughter's age, and was wearing very high heels and a tight, elegant red dress. It was like a scene from a film. Suddenly she turned her ankle on the cobblestones, and I overtook her as she paused to right herself. She was wiping tears from her eyes. Did the ankle twist hurt? A moment later I turned my head to see her running towards a handsome man and a gorgeous boy of about three. They all embraced. Tears sprang to my eyes as I watched them hugging one another, reuniting.

I was glad to leave Salamanca's historic centre. I realised that, for me, there's no point in visiting cities alone, though having come all this way it could be seen as a stupid waste to miss the opportunity. I know the buildings are grand and the history and culture inspiring, but it doesn't touch me; perhaps it's because I am ill, though I suspect it's because I am here for something quite different, though I don't yet know what that something is.

The next day I packed up, ready to leave Salamanca, and on the way out of town I swung by the megastore to return the adapter and to see if I could buy mosquito nets and chemical fluid for my loo. I couldn't find anyone who spoke English, so I had to mime these items. The mosquito net was quite easy. I knew *'fenêtre'*, which didn't ring any bells, so I made myself into a flying, buzzing insect and mimed a window, which did the trick and amused the assistant who directed me to a distant aisle. The inexpensive kit I found there was going to change my life on the road. I returned to the desk and asked the same woman about fluid for camping toilets. This was much more tricky. Puzzled, she called two colleagues over to help her decipher the request and all three watched as I attempted to describe, using only actions, a porta potti. They shook their heads in bewilderment. Whatever it was I wanted, they didn't think it was anything that might be for sale in their store. Eventually we had a breakthrough and they sent me to a partitioned display area, where stood an impressive array of porcelain bathroom suites. Sadly, I had no use – or space – for these luxurious delights in my van. Having embarrassed myself in front of three shop assistants and quite a few customers who had stopped to witness my performance, I was not prepared to leave empty-handed, and at last, after a long trek, I found the product about six feet along the aisle from the mozzie nets. I'd worked up quite a sweat, so I paid for my goods and walked out of the store and into the fresh morning air, then scuttled away comfortable in the knowledge that I would probably never see any of these good people again. Sometime later I discovered that a mosquito in Spanish is '*mosquito*.'

*

I have been following, rather slavishly, a route that seems logical if one wishes to get from Wales to the eastern end of the Algarve: one used by my friends who travel there regularly and by people I meet along the way who are chasing winter sun. It's a bit of a slog, because I am moving fairly slowly and I am not enjoying the sprawling city outskirts, or the motorways, or, for the most part, the landscape. That's fine –

it's a means to an end. But what about the *journey*? The journey is the point, isn't it? I look at the map. I am halfway along my route from northeast to southwest Spain, a journey that only takes some people a matter of hours, astonishingly.

If I divert and go west a bit, I can stay at an *aire* I spotted in my book, in the Sierra de Gata, which sounds like a wonderful place. Fear comes up and tries to make me play it safe, saying, 'Stick to the main roads; don't go up unnecessary mountains.' But this is nonsense; one road is much like another when you are driving along it – what does it matter if I take a scenic detour? So I head west and suddenly feel optimistic, and a little less nauseous.

The village of Torre de Don Miguel is slightly ramshackle and instantly lovable. The cobbled, narrow main street is entirely unsuitable for Myfanwy, but, thanks to Tanya, we take it anyway. It doesn't lead to the *aire,* which I find by using my own instinct. It's on the other side of a small valley and has a wonderful view of mountains and a distant ruined castle. I lock up and take the grassy footpaths around a patchwork of allotments, climbing the gentle hill to the edge of the village. A warren of back alleys eventually leads me to the main street where there's a small sloping plaza and, at the top, overlooking everything, an imposing church. Over the castellations of the tall, square tower, gargoyles lean out precariously, pulling menacing faces. Weeds grow in all directions, giving them wild, green hairdos which soften the gruesome effect a little. Beyond in the distance are more splendid forested mountains and another castle. Everything is green and lush in the afternoon sun. I feel I have entered another reality.

There are four bars in the square and I plump for 'Carpe Diem', because that is what I am trying to do: seize the day. I start to relax, enjoying sitting alone and lingering over a cold beer and olives in the warm evening sun. The square is quiet, apart from the chatter of a handful of people, the dull chime of the church bell at six o'clock and the occasional car rumbling up the cobbled street. Meandering back through the lanes to Myfanwy, I love what I see: layers of blue and green paint peeling off ancient doors, beautiful stonework, vegetable plots and olive groves. This is a place unspoilt by modernisation.

The following morning I get pulled back into my old pattern and rejoin the main road leading south to Caceres, just because that was the next place in my original plan. It's a city I am told I absolutely must visit. It's not a bad idea, but when I get there, I cannot face a walk around the scorching streets. I eat some dry bread and look at the map, willing it to show me what to do. It suddenly occurs to me that I don't have to doggedly follow the main road to Merida, then Zafra; I can head straight for Portugal, right now! Within minutes we are travelling due west, Myfanwy, Tanya and me. It's searingly hot and, happily, the fan works well, but Myfanwy's CD player is slightly damaged, and once I have managed to insert a disc it's nearly impossible to eject it. Consequently, I have had one CD on all the way through Spain. At first I was not sure if I liked this album, even though I am a big fan, but it went round and round so many times that I got to know it well and started to love it. Over a few days I learned all the words to Jamie Cullum's aptly named *Momentum* CD, and a lot of the lyrics seemed to resonate with me. Like Jamie, I feel I'm on the edge of something.

I start putting on a harmony here and there, accompanying Jamie as he accompanies me on my travels. It's so good to have a companion who sees the world a bit like I see it. We fly along,

I sing a lot and realise I am experiencing a new feeling – a good feeling. It's the absence of nausea, a returning strength in my body and joy. I am on the right road. Suddenly I am excited to be so close to the border where I will cross into the land which, for reasons unclear to me, I have dreamed of entering. I pull in at a supermarket. Outside is a large banner bearing my name, which seems a bit weird. Did they know I was coming? I go inside and over the loudspeakers they are playing the very same song I was just singing along to in the van. I do love a coincidence.

Part Two

I drive out of Spain and into Portugal, passing the derelict border control office. I am strangely moved. I have made it through Wales, England, France and Spain, and at last I am here in this place I have yearned to visit. I know so little about this country but I immediately see that it is beautiful. The houses are whitewashed, red-roofed and quaint, sitting on gentle slopes of green. In the distance I see an impressive hilltop castle, much like the Cathar castles of southwest France.

Before long I am climbing steeply up the winding road and the castle disappears behind trees. I continue twisting skywards at a snail's pace, then suddenly find I have arrived at the *aire*. I look out over the Alentejo plain, now stretched below me in the late afternoon sun: a patchwork of meadows in vivid russets and yellows, with gently pointed hills in the distance. I turn around and see that just above me is the spectacular castle. The village of Marvao is sheltered inside its ancient, hefty walls. I walk through a huge stone doorway and enter a higgledy-piggledy network of cobbled streets, with sweet white houses and terraces festooned with flowering plants. At first I get lost weaving through the confusion of narrow alleys, but I am able to retrace my own footsteps, gradually becoming familiar with this labyrinth of a place. I discover the main street, which looks just like all the other streets but has a shop and a post office. I find a bar and drink a much needed cold beer.

'Rain is coming,' the barman tells me, and minutes later, as I say goodbye and step onto the cobbles, a thick mist descends.

Within seconds visibility is down to a few feet. I guess we are quite high up here. The rain starts, as promised, and slowly drenches my inadequate clothing, which was appropriate for the climate only an hour ago. I know how easily walkers get disorientated in the fog on Welsh mountains, so I am glad that I am surrounded by castle walls. The scope for getting dangerously lost is actually quite limited here, yet the streets feel eerie and echoey, and I have no idea where I am going. I figure that as long as I keep to streets that descend, I will find my way back out of the misty maze. As I walk downhill, away from the castle, the cloud thins and I can just make out the shapes of the fields on the plain far below.

Back in the van I feel truly peaceful. I relax, allowing random images of the places I've been to so far to drift through my mind. Driving through Spain, I had such a strong urge to divert from the route I had thought I *should* be on: the main drag. And it did feel like a drag. Once I had given myself the freedom to follow my urge, a lot of things seemed to change – even the landscape, which suddenly became soft and beautiful. I was on smaller, friendlier roads, and as we went along I noticed myself singing heartily and talking to myself, and then laughing out loud for doing it. My decision to go west resulted in a rediscovery of joy. Finding Marvao and falling in love with it at first sight felt like a sign, confirming that I had made the right choice in following my heart. I often find myself wondering whether we create or simply follow the paths on which we travel through our lives, and whether we have a choice between creating and following. The idea that life is guiding me and showing me signs is intriguing and reassuring. It feels like a game that I can play if I dare.

I wake to the glorious sound of the bells from the convent

next to the *aire* and drink tea among my clothes, which are hanging out to dry in the van's open doorway. It rained heavily during the night and the thudding on the roof woke me, but I enjoyed it. I lay there and let my mind drift about, no longer plagued by the worries of earlier in the journey, which were – what? At first it was stressful, driving a van I didn't know on unfamiliar roads, following Tanya's instructions and fretting about where to stay each night, but that's all fading away now. I have cared too much for too long about a lot of things. I am not past caring, nothing so dramatic; I am just tired of worrying, bothering, minding. If minding means living life through the mind, then I have spent much of my life minding. It is only the mind that cares what happens. It always has a plan and it complains if things go awry. Driving along mostly empty roads these last few days, I find myself slipping out of my mind and into another place. Learning to trust and not worry about it all is something I have come to through practical experience, by driving right into and then beyond my fear. Really everything is just fine, flowing along, unfolding.

I drive south to Monsaraz, another small fortified city, whose walls are vast and brown. The place feels a little heavy and foreboding, not charming and inviting, as Marvao had appeared. Gazing out from this vantage point I can see the enormous *barragens*, or reservoirs, of Alentejo. It's a spectacular view, but I need to be somewhere less panoramic. I continue on to the next *aire,* twenty minutes south.

Luz is not panoramic or elevated or touristy. It's a new village, built to accommodate the people who once lived in a community which is now under dam water. The houses are single storey, all the same shade of white and with blue borders around the windows. The church is modern and compensates for its lack of maturity and grandeur by playing a hymn-like tune every half hour. It's a sweet sound, but wouldn't it drive you bananas after a few days? I need quiet and that is what I get, despite the church jingle – a place simply to rest my bones.

I have left all the secure things in my life to be here, in a car park next to a bull ring, overlooking a distant *barragem* on a cloudy day, far away from people I can talk to. I am known for talking a lot but I don't want to talk these days. I don't want to ask and answer questions. I am loving not having to interact – not having to do *anything*. I am following an invisible path, one that doesn't yet exist. I am here, present in the present. It occurs to me that I was often alone before, in my old life, but I was rarely still.

*

Myfanwy drives well and I have come to love her, despite minor failings. The cupboard doors are meant to slide, but they don't. I tug and shove and they come off in my hands. Sometimes they just jam stubbornly and I want to destroy them. Today, the crockery clatters ominously as I teeter along roads with crumbling edges and unforeseen potholes. It was Tanya's idea to take me on roads that are straight and direct but alarmingly narrow. I suspect they are Roman roads that have not been repaired much since Roman times. All of a sudden, she tells me to take the next turning, and we climb another mountain pass featuring endless bends and very few passing places. Thankfully, there's hardly any traffic. I sometimes wonder what would happen if I broke down out in the wilds, but then I stop wondering and focus on the fact that this is a game in which the challenge for me is to keep believing that everything is fine, and that if something goes wrong it will all work out in the end. Myfanwy seems to thrive on this adventure, and so do I. All this stretching is making us more flexible.

'Stay on this road for twenty-six miles,' Tanya commands. But, honestly, this is barely a road at all! Most of the time now I trust Tanya, although only yesterday we had a misunderstanding and I got furious with her. I shouted and swore at her, ending with the threat that I could turn her into an Irishman – which is quite easy to do, actually. I just select him from the menu and click. It's a strange world.

I drive through beautiful undulating countryside, drinking in the view. There are countless trees in neat rows that look like hi-vis baubles on sticks, the colour so iridescent that the whole scene is like a cartoon. Clouds gather and suddenly I am driving through a rainstorm. After a while I decide to stop battling through this poor visibility and pull in for a coffee break somewhere. As soon as I have this thought, a service station comes into view. I slow down, but the place is deserted except for a huge dog that stares at me sadly. I ask silently for a better option, and round the next bend a village appears with a cafe right by the road. The rain stops. A beautiful woman is standing in the canopied doorway. She must be seventy-something, I guess. Her dark brown face is crisscrossed with lines and she is tiny, very peaceful and still. She smiles, holding the door open for me. Her husband serves me coffee, which is very cheap and not bad.

As I am about to leave, the beautiful woman – who is not as tall as my shoulder – points to the sky and wags her crooked finger at me. It's bucketing down again. We stand under the awning outside the door, saying nothing for a good five minutes, listening to the deluge thudding onto the tarpaulin. Her comfortableness with silence is infectious. The rain passes and I smile and make to go, but she points to the oncoming weather: another big black cloud. Sure enough, there's another cloudburst and another lesson in stillness. The thudding gets even louder and we both start to laugh. We are two women, standing there, laughing at the rain, me feeling conspicuously tall and foreign. Finally I can leave. We look each other in the eye, and there's such a warmth in the silence. '*Obrigada*,' I say several times, as it is all the Portuguese I know – perhaps it's the only word I need right now. I *am* grateful. I love this place, its coffee, its people, the weather. Everything is so verdant and juicy and alive.

*

I arrive at my next stop, Alcoutim, which has a Spanish twin, Sao Lucas, across the Rio Guadiana: two whitewashed little towns each with a hilltop castle, and a ferry to connect them. I park next to a small caravan in the *aire* overlooking the town. An elderly man comes out to greet me, gently taking my hands in his as though we are old friends. He is Portuguese and speaks perfect English as he has travelled to England many times, taking the route that I have just travelled. He points to his little caravan and tells me that this has been his home ever since he took up a simple, nomadic life after his wife of sixty years died. 'Now it's just me and God,' he says, and sighs deeply. He smiles and directs me to a spot that he thinks I will enjoy, and he turns out to be right. At the other edge of the village is a river that has been dammed to make a swimming pool. The water is greenish but clean and warm. I have a wonderful swim in the afternoon sunshine. I wonder if the lovely caravan man is a sort of self-elected host, warmly welcoming all the travellers who come his way.

After my swim I wander down through the village to the riverside, where there are a few bars and cafes. I choose one with a terrace and sit sipping wine, drinking in the atmosphere and the view across the wide, glassy river in the diminishing evening light. All at once the village across the river is twinkling with white street lights; moments later a string of orange street lamps comes to life along Alcoutim's riverfront. Just behind me, the church bell chimes seven times; a second later, across the water, in Spain, I hear the eight o'clock bells.

The next day, after a good lunch costing very little (my first meal for days), I follow the Guadiana downstream almost to its mouth and head west towards the home of my friends from Wales. I have no address, just scribbled directions and some incomplete-looking coordinates, which I put into Tanya's brain. We come off the motorway onto a small road, continuing along even smaller roads and then tiny lanes through fields of crops. I have no idea where we are and I realise I have lost my innate sense of direction, having handed over all control to sat nav. I also notice I am getting dangerously low on fuel. According to Tanya I am very close to my destination, but this must be wrong, because I am nowhere. We have come away from civilisation across a landscape that means nothing to me, so I resort to checking my written directions. I saw no village square, no wash house; none of the landmarks I was meant to pass along the way. There's only thirty yards to go according to the small screen, but the houses petered out a while ago.

My friends had told me to call them if I got lost and they would come and get me. But how could I explain my position except *lost*? All the lanes look the same. Twenty yards, ten yards… this feels bad. I round a slight bend in the road.

'You have reached your destination,' Tanya announces. But there's nothing here. I have no choice but to continue to the next turning place. A few moments later there's another bend, then a wall and a rusty blue gate, half obscured with trailing jasmine. Good old Tanya! She has got me to a hidden house in a remote place via a route that felt like a wild goose chase. I assume this must be the house. There's nobody around so I let myself in through the gate, calling, 'Hellooooo!' I sit in the garden and wait, and twenty minutes later we are together in the right place. There's a lot of hugging and grinning and, on my part, relief. Mugs of tea are handed round.

The house is typically Portuguese: single storey, whitewashed and built more for function than aesthetics, yet pretty in a simple way. The flat roof is used for al fresco sleeping in the summer. The kitchen is a lean-to across a little yard. Outside the front door is a terrace, shaded by a vine-covered pergola. There are plants everywhere: jasmine and passionflower cascade over the outdoor bread oven; rosemary and lavender scent the yard while honeysuckle and bougainvillea cover its high walls. A path leads up through the semi-wild garden, past a compost loo, to a small self-built pool. The location is very rural and quiet, yet only about half an hour from the sea.

My hosts Martin and Catherine have lived in Pembrokeshire for decades, where I see them from time to time, and now spend increasing portions of the year here, in this offbeat part of the Algarve. They are older than me: a laidback, long-married couple. Martin is the owner of a wild, white mop of hair and matching beard, and he's a fine guitarist and singer.

He's always been very sweet to me, encouraging me to sing and demanding that I learn tricky harmonies that sound beautiful against his softly sung melodies. I can't remember exactly how I first met him but it must have been in the nineties, almost certainly at a folk club or a small festival in west Wales where we would both have been performing. It seems like another life, and I can only bring to mind fragments and vague images of those days. During my stay Martin reminded me that he used to play in a prog rock covers band with Peter, my friend and ex-partner and the father of my two children. That was back in the glorious seventies, a decade before I met Peter. Somehow I'd forgotten they even knew each other.

In the early eighties, at sixteen tender years old, I flew the nest and made my escape from Cardiff. I moved in a small clockwise circle around England, apprenticing and working in craft potteries. I loved the work, but I began to realise I didn't belong in any of the places where I lived – they just didn't feel like home – and ended up staying in Oxford, near my brother who lived there. I was trying to work out what to do with my life. I became immersed in the city's lively folk scene, and it was through music that I got to know Peter. Over a couple of years we became close friends, then got together. Neither of us were Oxford students – we just happened to be there for a while. He was planning a move back to Wales – also his homeland – and, ironically for me, settled on Cardiff as his destination. And it was now my destination, too, as I belonged with Peter, regardless of geographical preferences. Peter was my rock – true to his name.

Somewhat reluctantly I returned to my city roots – living only a few miles from my broken family home was not what

I'd had in mind – and we bought a tiny terraced house on a treeless street in Splott. Deep down my dream had been to venture much further west, shunning urban life altogether. I had to wait another fifteen years before we made that move. Meanwhile, we were a good team, and precious years flew by as we raised our two children, renovated our house and succeeded in making a very modest living in the arena of music and the arts. Finally, after a lot of discussion, we did move to the wild west of Wales, and, almost immediately, our relationship came apart. This was something we hadn't factored into our plans, and we handled it as best we could. Over time, new partners came into our lives and we remained friends, continuing to work together as parents and on various musical projects. We still do.

Now here I am in Portugal, looking back on a long, long journey full of twists and turns. There's sadness in nostalgia, but there's also comfort in continuity – it feels good to see how it is all connected.

I didn't meet Catherine until relatively recently. I knew of her existence, but she had always seemed slightly mysterious. She wasn't part of the music scene and had her own interests, which included spending as much time as possible in the Algarve, often leaving Martin back home to continue with his job. Now he has retired they both love to be here as much as possible, enjoying the climate, the culture and the people. I am so glad I've come to know Catherine, because I love spending time with her. She is simply a beautiful, peaceful woman and we get on really harmoniously, as though we have been friends for decades.

Two other friends from Pembrokeshire are also here, staying for a week. Chris is a keen cook, which is a bonus. He is a good friend of David's and mine and he has brought Alys with him, who I guess is in her early thirties, much younger than him. I've not met Alys before and it's hard to tell if they are an item. If they are, it must have happened recently; last time we saw Chris, only a few weeks ago, he was definitely single.

I tell them about my journey and they tell me about the weather, which has been unusually wet for the last week and has turned everything a fresh green and caused delicate, pretty weeds to grow up through the gravel all over the yard. They bring me up to date on all the things they've been up to: mostly swimming, relaxing, shopping for fresh fish in the market, and eating – it sounds wonderful.

*

For two days I have enjoyed companionship, bathroom facilities, great cooking and a lovely place to be. I have burst out of the bubble of my independence and I am now part of a group, weighing up how to fit in and be a helpful guest. I have changed mode and mood, talking more than I have for weeks. I relax and my appetite returns. Something is gained, but something is lost, too. I feel nostalgic thinking that the magical atmosphere, created by being only with myself, my van and my one CD, might never return. It's strange: now that I am no longer alone, I feel incomplete. I miss David and a vague insecurity arises, as though I have lost some of the strength that manifested itself because I had no choice but to look after myself. Have I left part of me somewhere along the road, abandoned?

It rains on and off for five days. We are philosophical about it, agreeing that, although we would love to lounge about in the sun, rain is something to be grateful for.

'Being Welsh, we can handle this sort of weather – as long as it's accompanied by tea and cakes,' Martin says. He has brought in supplies of *pastéis de nata,* Portuguese custard tarts, which everyone loves. We all know each other fairly well, apart from Alys, and she is pretty laidback. There is an easy companionship between us all.

Sometimes we play Scrabble, sitting on the terrace under a canopy. In the warm evenings we talk, eat and drink excellent Portuguese wine. We visit local towns, markets, cafes and a wonderful restaurant in Tavira, a town not far away, built on both banks of a tidal estuary and connected by bridges. It is both elegant and unpretentious, with fishermen bringing in their catch just a stone's throw from the smart, newly refurbished plaza.

One day, my friends suggest a yoga class in a nearby town, and I decide to go along, though I haven't done any yoga for about ten years. The teacher is a firm, business-like woman of sixty-something. After some stretching and breathing, she gives each of us a small stack of foam blocks to help us with our headstands. I know I won't be able to do this. She comes over and I tell her not to waste time on me, and that I'll sit this one out. But she is quite sure I am going to do it. I am worried that this will put my neck out, but she gets me semi-inverted with the blocks under my hips in no time and suddenly I am completely upside down. It feels wonderful! I stay there for what feels like a long time in an effortless headstand, seeing the world from a new perspective. After the session, I feel that I have indeed stretched myself, mostly just by saying 'yes' to something I could easily have rejected as being contradictory to my commitment to idleness.

The next afternoon was slightly weird. I decided to tag along to a clairvoyance circle, which some local friends of my hosts had joined very enthusiastically. We went in the spirit of openness and without cynicism, but we took some salt, too, so that we could take a pinch at any time, if needed. Where clairvoyance is concerned, I find myself a bit sceptical. Even if there is a message, it won't be for me.

Einstein said that 'everything in life is vibrating,' and that what we call 'matter' is actually energy. Nothing stays still – even seemingly solid things like tables. I feel the energy in my own body. I know myself to be in a state of constant movement, however tiny those movements are. Otherwise, I guess I'd be dead. But even then, my body would change and become part of the ever-evolving environment. What about my consciousness? Would it continue vibrating? How would I know?

I think we all sense changes in human vibrations. We feel the subtle force of what is going on inside another's being without a word being spoken. Through practice, perhaps we can begin to recognise and filter the data. It's only when we communicate our findings that we get feedback and find out if they are accurate. I guess this is what clairvoyants do, either by reading the person in the room or picking up something emitted from those who have ceased to be alive. The idea that dead relatives are sending messages to the living could be a load of hokum, yet it's not unusual to experience instances of suddenly knowing something previously unknown. Sometimes information seems to come from nowhere, or somewhere beyond the mind, as if everything that has ever happened is stored out there in a cloud to be brought into use as needed. Still – I was sure that there would no messages for me.

During the session I wondered if there was a slight

desperation to fit messages to people in the room. At one point, Bert, a keen trainee clairvoyant, reported that he was seeing large cloths, which were draped over what looked like fences – possibly to dry. He said this was taking place in Yorkshire.

'Anyone have relatives from Yorkshire?' asked the group's teacher, Dilys.

I kept quiet. Bert went on:

'It's definitely Yorkshire, and there are all these huge cloths, like blankets; some of them are dark.' I asked if they were made of wool, and Bert said he thought they might be. I started to think of my grandfather's woollen mill in Yorkshire. Did they hang large pieces of woollen cloth out to dry, or something? I wondered. It occurred to me that perhaps he was seeing the frames where the woven fabric was displayed, so that the menders could examine them for defects. My mother used to tell me about the 'invisible menders' and their incredible skill. As a child, I thought she was talking about people who were actually invisible, like the shoemaker's elves. 'Does anyone here relate to that?' Dilys asked. Again I kept shtum. After a pause, she said: 'I'm getting a word very strongly... yes, it's clear now... it's "picture." Yes, that's it: picture – I have no idea why.'

Picture? Pitcher! My grandfather's name was Pitcher. Oh no! I had to own up.

'It's me!' I confessed. 'I had relatives in Yorkshire, lots of them. My mother's whole family came from Yorkshire.'

Dilys shot me a slightly irritated look. I told her about my grandfather's name, and she said, 'Did he have a lot of trauma in his life?'

'Yes,' I said, but didn't everybody? My grandfather; his name; his woven woollen cloth; Yorkshire. I had to admit that my attention had been grabbed.

Bert said the message was for me. 'Whatever is happening now, however difficult things have been, the important thing is *after that*. After that. There's nothing to fear; something significant will happen... hang in there, because *after that* is the important thing.'

After the long session I couldn't wait to get away, and we left feeling 'a bit queer', as my Yorkshire grandma would have called it. Was that really a message meant for me? I never knew my maternal grandfather; he died a few years before I was born. Was he looking out for me? Had he been watching my life unfold from some other realm? If so, he would have seen me walk a pretty troubled road. His own life had not been easy, surviving, as he had, his father's untimely death, great poverty, service in the First World War and the death of his twenty-nine year old son, among other things. He must have been a strong character, just as my mother had said. He would have understood some of my tribulations. I wish I had known him.

After arriving back at the house I went to get something from the van and the heavy sliding side door came off in my hands, nearly knocking me over. Was this significant – symbolic? A door opening that cannot be closed? What did it mean? Probably nothing more than the fact that the van was old and rusty – but I was experiencing an eerie sense that every little thing could be a message, just for me. That night, I felt a lot of old stuff from my past surfacing. As I drifted in and out of sleep I felt the presence of a friend who had died some years before. I wasn't sure if it was a dream, but it was as if she was right there in the van, visiting me, standing close to me, larger than she'd been in life and translucent. She was very calm and seemed to be communicating with me without speaking. What did she want to say? As I focussed, her presence subsided and

I was left only with the feeling that she was at peace. It was as though she had come to tell me that I needn't carry any despair about her and the violent way she had ended her own existence. I'd felt guilty that I had not been able to help her – though I tried, as did all her loved ones. But now that guilt had gone.

Next morning, I awoke to find maggots crawling around my cooker, which I hadn't used since arriving as I had been eating with my friends on their terrace. There was no food in the van, so it was easy to clear up the creatures and clean the tiny kitchen area. Still, I have a slight phobia of maggots, and it gave me 'the willies' – another granny word. Was this retribution for killing all those flies a couple of weeks before? Maybe not, but it was probably the result of their invasion. Things improved as my friends and I spent the day walking, swimming in the sea and playing music together. I forgot about maggots and messages from the other side. We also went to a local garage to get my door fixed. The mechanic was really helpful and friendly, and did his best to make a temporary repair, for which he wanted to charge me a few euros. Amusingly, I had to argue with him that it was too cheap. Later David rang and told me the sad news that a friend from our village had died – she was not much older than me. Though expected, it still came as a shock. I felt sad and very far away from home.

I am noticing that the more I talk, the more off-centre I become. It is subtle now, whereas in my youth it was hard not to feel spun-out a lot of the time. I love the sharing that goes on between the five of us here, but there comes a point where I begin to feel self-conscious again. I seem to become someone I am no longer sure is really me – a person I don't really like, who might be competitive or show off or talk too much, when what I really want is to be quiet and do nothing. We have been singing songs together accompanied by banjo and guitar, which I love, and yet, I want a break from even this gentle and nurturing activity. I notice the mantra in my head: 'Must do, must keep doing.' That is exactly what I want to break with.

*

For the first time in a while, I start to sleep through the night: six or seven hours of deep sleep. How different it feels! Those wakeful hours between three and five can seem such a waste of time. I try to stay relaxed and to manage my mind as it starts to whizz. Thanks to Eckhart Tolle and others, like J. Krishnamurti, I am learning to handle it better. I watch the mind, knowing that, contrary to appearances, it is not me and I am not it.

This morning I am enjoying a really good pot of tea, thanks to David having sent reinforcements with Chris. The making and drinking of tea is a big enough activity for a sleepy October morning. Tea is a serious subject – sometimes a controversial one. Tea must be made properly. The pot must be warmed thoroughly and the water has to be at a rolling boil as it's poured onto good quality tea, preferably loose-leaf. And then it's all about time. The pot must be covered with a cosy and left to brew for five minutes. Welsh water, generally speaking, is ideal for making tea, due to its softness. There is, of course, the question of milk, and that's another thorny issue. I have had to get used to UHT milk – it's a matter of survival.

Sometimes the topic of tea can precipitate heated discussion in the domestic arena. David has said he thinks I am a tiny bit obsessional about it. It's true that I tend to supervise or even micro-manage the process. Well, it's important to me. Actually, he makes a perfect cup of tea.

In my life, tea has evolved from a simple beverage into a ritual, even a sacred ceremony. More than anything, it is a time of total avoidance and indulgence. Some people naturally take the time they need for relaxation and enjoyment; others of us have had to learn this necessary art. My method is to avoid, when possible, all contact with anyone between waking and finishing my third cup of tea. Never cram three cups into a few minutes. Time is crucial.

Now I gaze upon the cracked white teapot and beyond it, to the still misty world outside: a reality distinct from the cocoon of my duvet and my solitude, where I am slowly coming alive as I progress from zero to three cups in approximately forty-five minutes.

From my earliest memory, I was catapulted, like so many other children, from deep sleep into the realm of *doing,* with no time for adjustment. I cannot know what effect this has had on others, though I suspect there's a correlation between this and the state the world is in. For me, the pause between sleep and activity is sacrosanct. After all, what is sleep? Where do we go? What happens there? Are we changed, recharged, reset or returned to something? Sleep might be so much more than just a rest from all we do. It could be a journey to another realm – 'time out of mind,' as Bob Dylan might say. It is the mind that keeps us from sleep, and sleep that frees us from the mind. The computer is off – so what is operating the system?

Back to tea: I am feeling so glad and grateful to have slept well that I am celebrating with a second pot. This is the advanced level. Not everyone is capable of a long sit. The mistake a lot of 'spiritual seekers' make is to believe that they have to be uncomfortable or get up in the dark, say three a.m., to *sit*. I am sitting in my warm bed, however, at nine thirty, with my huge duvet wrapped around me, and I don't even have to leave my bed to make the tea. The possibilities for indulgence are much enhanced in a little camper van like mine. Later I might well be in a suitable state to meet other humans, even to stay relaxed and centred when talking happens. My brain will be empty, receptive, calm. I won't feel grumpy.

In my little van I can indulge one hundred per cent my needs and desires, which are silence, time and tea. Anyone who thinks I am lazy simply misses the point. Those who envy me get the point, but fail to understand the work that has gone into gaining this ability to listen to my soul. It was extremely difficult for me to find peace, to know what I needed, to give myself any space at all. The pressures and constraints that modern life inflicts upon humankind were pressing hard on me. In a way, it was lucky that I cracked under the pressure and collapsed. I had no choice but to rest, and it took years to learn to live, to be, and to resist the urge to try to snap back into the old shape, or to rehabituate myself into the mode I had known and been trained in.

In order to ensure I have the space I need every morning, I employ a bit of rebranding to help people to feel really good about not disturbing me, and to make me feel righteous about avoidance. I tell them: 'I must do my meditation first thing, and I'll see you later.' What I leave unsaid is: 'Do not disturb me or judge me as a lazy slug, a shirker or a habitual hangover-sufferer.' Everyone seems happy with the meditation label, or at least willing to indulge my indulgence.

*

Today has gone quickly. I left my dear Welsh friends at midday and drove north through the Algarve hinterland, which involved lots of ups and downs for Myfanwy. A few hours later, I arrived at Bob and Jenny's place, which I had found on the internet. It rests on a plateau in a range of small mountains like little volcanoes, and is very pretty. The recent ten days of rain have made everything very lush and green. I was welcomed and shown around a basic campsite with taps that didn't work and no loos. The hub of the community was a plastic marquee. This makeshift building was where food was stored and cooked. There was a small table with chairs over which hung a single light bulb, which attracted all manner of flying bugs at dusk. It was a practical solution, though not a beautiful one. My hosts had offered food and somewhere to camp in exchange for work improving their site. It was not clear exactly what this place was going to be, neither to me nor to its owners when I asked them. It was work in progress. There was one other voluntary worker staying: a handsome young Portuguese man, Felipe. I found a spot and set up camp, then joined the others for dinner. Apart from the four of us, there were dogs who were in charge of guarding their home, and after barking a lot when I tried to approach the marquee, they settled down and we became friends. It was a convivial evening, and I felt comfortable and welcome. After enjoying food and wine with my new friends, I picked my way through the pitch dark and the scrub along the stony path to my van, which felt very much like home.

*

I wake in the middle of the night from dreams which are mundane, yet strangely powerful in their ability to grip my psyche. I open my curtains whilst still lying in bed and through the tall back doors I see more stars than I have seen for years – even decades. They are bright enough to illuminate the moonless night. Some constellations are huge and complex, appearing only in the periphery of my vision. When I look at them directly they are invisible. Gazing at the night sky makes me think about the philosophy of the music of the spheres, and the science of the harmonic series. That leads to thinking about all the things that seem fixed – the firmament, mathematics, the laws of physics and nature – and things that seem changeable – our evolution as a species and as individuals, and the way we transform our environment and language over time. In fact, nothing rests. Everything is moving, always.

Music is sensual, emotional, yet it belongs in the realm of mathematics. We make patterns using the fixed physics of music – scales, pitch, intervals – either consciously or unconsciously. Everything is vibrating; that is what physics tells us. Human beings can attune, creating change in vibration through singing, chanting, meditation, and so on. Perhaps we are the only lifeform on Earth that can make that choice. That is a pretty amazing thought, even though it might be inaccurate. Gazing into the heavens changes my perspective. All of life seems so completely magical. At three in the morning, my mind can ramble like this and it all makes perfect sense. Eventually I fall back to sleep, and I wake once the sun has already reached its mid-morning position.

The van is hot and airless. I wake with a question: am I getting homesick? The truth is, I have not felt homesick at all so far. I have missed almost no one and nothing. Nourished by the warm sunshine and new vistas and occupied by the whole business of being on the road, I have a lot to fill up my senses. The days go by quickly and I rarely find myself idle for long. I feel great love and appreciation for my family and friends, and even wish that they could share all this, or part of it. I miss the comfort of my partner and the familiarity of our relationship, but at the same time I enjoy the freedom to think only of myself, to drop the mind with its nagging voice urging me attend to what others might need, might want, might think of me. I am free of the urge to appease, please and gain approval. So, I don't feel homesick right now, but I recognise that there's a state I have found myself in a lot throughout my life: I have longed for home. But what home? Where? Maybe I have longed for something else – something I don't even know. Perhaps I yearn to find a sense of belonging, sanctuary and peace, in the way one can long to fall in love. It is not a person I miss but a state; a state I don't experience but recognise all the same.

Now I begin to understand that this sense of belonging does not exist in a particular location, building or person, but is rooted inside my being, regardless of where, when or with whom I find myself. Interestingly, I am starting to find it easier to remain rooted in this state whilst travelling alone, without much of a plan or destination. I am finding something deeply peaceful and secure in what Joni Mitchell calls the 'refuge of the roads.' I leave home and find home in every place and no place – and, perhaps, within my self.

*

I have been here for several days, working as best I can to help Felipe level a sloped area using pickaxes and shovels. The work ethic is relaxed and I am required to contribute only a few hours each day. When I haven't been up half the night, stargazing and philosophising, I rise early and get ready to start work at nine, when the air is cool. I wait around for signs of life, which manifest in the form of birds and other creatures who I can hear more than see. But there's never any sign of Bob and the breakfast he has promised: a banquet of scrambled eggs, ham, cheeses, breads and coffee. As the time passes, I try to sit in a state of blissful meditation and watch the morning come into focus as the sun rises and the mist magically disperses, exposing the solid yet soft landscape.

This is a special time of day. It is profoundly peaceful and I have it all to myself, yet all I can think about is that breakfast: the warm softness of the scrambled eggs, the steaming coffee and comforting bread. The expectation of breakfast and the knowledge that I need some energy to do my work combine to make me feel slightly anxious. I am keeping to someone else's timetable, but it has not come to anything concrete. Perhaps it was merely an idea, an intention. I have taken it literally and feel slightly peeved.

After a few days, I stop setting my alarm clock, lie in bed until I feel like rising and arrive later each morning. The breakfast never materialises and we generally start work at lunchtime, when the sun is high and the temperature almost prohibitive. Felipe says he is acclimatised, so he doesn't mind toiling through what I understand to be siesta time.

I find the combination of physical effort and intense heat makes me unable to work except in short bursts, interspersed with rests in the shade. Mad dogs and Englishmen! – or, in this case, a possibly slightly mad Englishman whose ideas are not matched by his actions, running things in a somewhat ad hoc way. The dogs seem very sensible and keep out of the heat and the work area. Lunch eventually appears at about three in the afternoon, by which time I feel weak with hunger and heat exhaustion.

Yesterday evening, I discovered a hornet's nest in the tree right next to my van and promptly moved. My new location is higher, prettier and not next to a hornets' nest, as far as I can tell. I start to relax and enjoy my lazy mornings, drinking tea outside my van with the horses that visit to eat acorns right outside my door, and gradually let go of the fantasy breakfast, satisfied instead with some muesli I find in my cupboard.

*

Today, Felipe and I were driven by Bob to a local town. A short scenic tour was given, though there wasn't much to see, and we did a supermarket shop and recycling drop-off. This took up the whole long, boiling afternoon. It wasn't really what I needed – a swim in a cold lake would have been more my cup of tea. On the way home I felt irritable as I was captive in Bob's car, listening to one of his rambling monologues. I stared out of the window, wondering what I was doing here. I can imagine how I must have appeared. I am sure Bob notices my body language, which could be interpreted as disinterested at the very least. Anyway, at least I had picked up some more muesli and milk.

Bob is full of enthusiasm and ideas. He likes to talk about the way he sees the world and tell stories about past volunteers, some of which might be better left unsaid. What on earth will he say about me to future visitors? I know he means well, but his conversation tends to be rather one-way; he has no interest in me – or in Felipe for that matter, though Felipe doesn't seem to mind. He is young and tolerant, whereas I feel I am becoming a grumpy old woman. Perhaps I am simply a fish out of water here.

It's not that I don't like to hear stories; I do enjoy a good yarn, and I find myself remembering Gilbert. A few years ago, when David and I were travelling in the Pyrenées, we had been given a contact, a must-see guy called Gilbert, whose long, golden hair was remarkable considering he was well into his sixties. From the moment we arrived as strangers at his ramshackle home, complete with extensive menagerie, he regaled us with stories about his many years as a roadie for some of the world's top rock bands. Though he never divulged a name or broke a confidence, he generously shared anecdotes and described incredible journeys and antics that kept us entertained for hours every evening and late into the night. He confessed that he didn't cook, so we took care of shopping and preparing meals. He also told us he didn't really drink alcohol, but the three of us worked our way through his drinks cabinet, which had been remarkably well-stocked when we arrived. The hours would race by as we sat in rapt attention night after night, until it was time for us to move on and we left, filled up with his wondrous stories. He thanked us for helping him empty his drinks cabinet. After all, he didn't really drink.

*

I find myself longing to get away. I guess I had made up a picture in my mind of a small, random collection of fellow travellers who would work together, sharing skills and roadtrip anecdotes. We would achieve something worthwhile and hang out, swim, drink cold beer and generally have a fabulous time. I feel a slight disappointment, which is the sum of expectation plus reality. It would be nice to have a bit of female company. I like Jenny; she is thoughtful and interesting, and I wish there were more opportunities to talk with her, but she is always busy elsewhere, with her own work.

This place is Bob and Jenny's dream. It is wild and beautiful, but it will be a while before it has the kind of facilities that might be expected by the paying guest, and I am glad I am not paying. It has potential, though when I hear my hosts describing what they have created here, it seems to me a little rose-tinted. There was once a decent track, but it got washed away in a rainstorm, and as quickly as they clear a patch of ground, the waist-high weeds take over again. They seem to have lost momentum, postponing projects for one reason or another. It appears that they are losing a race to get ahead and manage their wilderness. I suspect that secretly they want to gift their land back to nature and forget any ideas about landscaping, vegetable plots, easy access and guests.

It takes a lot of time and energy to realise the dream of the 'good life' and to maintain the land. I know of couples back home who sought to create a romantic natural idyll, living off the land and solar energy, but ended up isolated, impoverished, at the end of an unnavigable track and their tethers enduring winters which drove them to drink, or insane, or both. That won't happen here, I'm sure, but I feel that if I stay here much longer, I might succumb to a mild madness. Well, at least the Portuguese winter is fairly clement most of the time, and I wish Bob and Jenny the best of luck anyway.

*

Again I have woken at four in the morning, this time with a strong sense that it's time to move on. I realise that I am marking time and that the frustration I feel has less to do with being wide awake in the middle of the night and more to do with an awareness that I must not ignore. Though I have enjoyed being here, I am no longer willing to risk sunstroke while grafting in the midday heat. It's not for me. Bob and Jenny offered me a lot of freedom – they were welcoming and easygoing – but I need even more freedom than I can allow myself to have whilst being their guest. I long for freedom as though I have never had it. I go out once again to view the stars in a sky free from light pollution. The night is spectacular, with shooting stars in the south and the Milky Way stretching across the heavens. My insomnia has at least given me this opportunity – a gift from life. It's just me and the stars.

*

This evening, I am sitting alone in my van in a place that I chose for a few reasons: it has a swimming pool, a bar and other people, hopefully of like minds. Also, it happens to be a naturist campsite, which appeals to my desire to soak up as much autumn sun as possible. I have lounged naked on nude beaches before, so it isn't a problem for me in theory, but it's been a while since I last walked around unclothed in front of people. There's also the question of temperature. It has been very hot for the past few weeks, but I am told cooler weather is on its way tomorrow. Anyway, it's dark now, and I have closed myself in for the night. I am very, very tired.

It's seven o'clock in the morning. The clocks went back last night, so it's now six, but it doesn't *feel* like six. Messing with relative time is confusing and disconcerting. The sun has just come up through some fairly half-hearted, wispy clouds. Yesterday I had a disaster. Moving Myfanwy off my peaceful spot at Bob and Jenny's, I had not secured the cupboards properly. To be honest, the doors are so stubborn and difficult to slide that I have to restrain myself from yanking them off altogether and flinging them out of the window. I didn't secure the top cupboards, nor did I replace the top on the bottle of water, which I had also failed to tie down. I was caught up in the excitement of moving on. As I lurched round and down the winding dirt track back towards what people call civilisation I heard the sound of clattering dishes. That was nothing to worry about; I am used to it – they are usually all noise and no action. What I didn't hear was my precious supply of Clipper teabags flying through the air into a puddle making its way silently across the floor. I now have the sombre task of counting how many fit-for-purpose, sun-dried teabags remain, then making an estimate of the time I have here in Portugal before reinforcements might arrive along with David. It's close – too close for comfort – and we could be looking at an alarming deficit. That is to say, there might be a few days when I can only use one teabag instead of two or three. I hope I'll survive.

*

I so want to hear from David; it has been a while since we've spoken on Skype or by phone. I feel a little isolated, far away from him and from home. I hope this feeling will soon pass along with the clouds that are filling the sky today. I imagined resting in the warm sunshine and swimming, but it's a little bit chilly. I would like to meet some people I can talk and laugh with. At the end of my stay at Bob and Jenny's, I took Felipe out for lunch. We shared a huge pot of Portuguese fish stew, a bottle of wine and a great deal of laughter. I wonder if I should feel guilty. Both 'should' and 'guilty' are words I would rather not entertain, but I find myself asking the question nonetheless. I haven't laughed that much for ages, and I have no idea what we were even laughing about. If David was dining with a beautiful young woman I might feel a little insecure, but being on the road, companionship is necessary and I take it in whatever form it comes. I know I can be friends with a man without romance or passion entering into it, but I wonder if Felipe feels differently. We might hook up for another lunch in a nearby cafe – he said he would be passing this way in the next week or so – or we might never meet again. Either way, I hope I did not lead him on, however unwittingly.

*

Apart from the teabag trauma, things are going swimmingly. The weather has improved enough for just about everyone here to go about their business in their birthday suits. It would have felt weird to be different, and I, too, have been going around completely naked. At first, I had to adjust to that feeling that something was missing. It's funny how, every now and then, I have a sudden panic, wondering if I have made a mistake and simply forgotten to dress, so that I have to have a quick look around to check that I am not the only naked person at a campsite full of clothed people. That would be embarrassing, and the stuff of bad dreams – though, when I really think it through, why should it be? Clothing the body is as peculiar as leaving it in its natural, unclothed state, if not more so – though living in Wales, it would be inadvisable to be a hard-line, full-time naturist. There are a few days each year, usually in June, when it might be bearable to strip off, but it's a rare treat. Anyway, the people here are definitely nude, and I am comfortable in nothing but my skin. I find it useful to employ the rule of climbing ladders: just don't look down. So far, everyone seems truly friendly, making good eye contact and including me in whatever is going on. I think I am going to like being here for a while: reading, writing, swimming and, at last, relaxing.

*

It's Wednesday – not a great favourite of mine. Wednesday often feels like a low point in the week, imbued with the threat of woe. I can't charge my laptop because there's not enough solar power, so I have no music. The sliding door came sliding off the van again; this time, it whacked me on the head and caused me to sprain my wrist. I got the door back on with the help of two naked men, but now it is locked closed. I can't Skype, because the signal here is so unreliable. I did have a good day, though. I swam and played Scrabble with a sweet English couple I met, who invited me for coffee and then lunch, to which I took a bottle of wine and some snacks. I finished the book I was reading and did a crossword. Swatting flies has been an absorbing activity, too. I wish I could talk properly with David.

What is going on? There's no Wi-Fi now; it has gone, totally, in the whole place. Someone said the satellite has gone AWOL – the satellite? The malfunctioning Wi-Fi took my phone out, too, as I was connected to it at the time. I tried turning it off and on – that cure-all – but to no avail. This means I am totally out of contact. Is Mercury in retrograde? That might explain these strange happenings. I did want to get away from it all, but it's slightly unnerving to be out of touch. How quickly we have come to depend on technology! I seem to have little challenges to deal with every few days. I wonder who or what is challenging me?

*

Thanks to a kind Irishman who lent me an adapter, I have electricity now, and though my side door is locked shut, I can access the van by swivelling round on the 'captain's seat' at the front, which is quite fun. In fact, I have all I need here, not only the basics, I have luxury too. Last night I had a sauna, and a new couple arrived to camp in the spot where the English couple had been. I joined in with a large group for dinner at a long communal table in the bar. It felt good to be part of a friendly gathering of people from all over Europe. We were all dressed on this occasion.

I haven't heard from Felipe, and now we have no way of getting in touch. It might have been nice to go out for lunch but don't really mind whether he comes or not. I just feel bad that he might be trying to contact me. He could be slowly losing his mind at Bob and Jenny's, still chipping away with his pickaxe and no breakfast inside him. I guess he can look after himself, though.

The new couple who arrived look like a pair of golden angels, or fairies – I am not sure which. They are Swedish, both musicians, and speak perfect English. It feels as though we have some common ground. They helped me by letting me use their mobile internet, so I was able to send an email out to let my friends at home know about my communications problems.

*

It's been a good week. I have rested and the Wi-Fi is back on. The Swedish angels and I have been playing music, singing songs and discussing philosophy. I am sad to find that they are only staying a few days, but we have said we'll try to hook up somewhere along the way. There's another kindred spirit here: Jan is a sweet soul, gentle and troubled. In fact, he's been broken-hearted since his long marriage hit the rocks, and he has come here to find space and peace away from his broken home. He overheard my end of a difficult conversation via Skype and afterwards he told me what had happened to him.

'Twenty-seven years and two children, and now she says it's all over. But why? She can't tell me why, and I love her,' he said. As he shared his story, he started to cry. I listened and held his hand for a while, and then I started crying too.

I had finally talked with David, but the conversation had been surprisingly awkward – an argument, really. Earlier in the year, it had seemed a real possibility that we would make this entire trip together – at least, that's how I remember it. However, in the spring, our six-year relationship had become decidedly rocky, and our issues remained unresolved as I left on my solo adventure. David had promised to come and see me for a short visit, even though we were not sure whether we would stay together in the long term.

Our relationship had never been a particularly romantic one. I suspect that we both wondered how and why we had come to be sharing this part of our lives, as the futures we each envisaged were not all that compatible. When we met, neither of us was in a great place – we were both recuperating from past unhappiness and a bit lost. Our jagged edges didn't fit together comfortably to form one smooth, rounded entity. The first few years of our partnership were peppered with occasions when we couldn't agree on how and where to make a home together. It was a scab that we picked at from time to time.

What we shared were similar core values, a willingness to talk about absolutely anything, and an appreciation of hedonism and Scrabble. Time went on and we rubbed along together quite nicely most of the time, possibly in the knowledge that we were somehow meant to be together. With hindsight, I can see that our sharp edges had been gradually worn away. We had become entwined and familiar, like family. We were living in a tiny rented cottage. At last we'd found somewhere we could settle, and so we'd created a productive vegetable garden. The location was perfect. Life was sweet.

Last spring we hit a rough patch. Both of us had been profoundly unsettled by something outside our control: our landlady had decided to leave her job and convert our cottage into holiday accommodation. The perennial issue of our living circumstances suddenly came into sharp focus, this time dividing us. Though we talked, we were not really getting to the nitty gritty of our problem, or any closer to a solution. Accommodation in our part of Pembrokeshire is hard to come by. Harbouring and perhaps hiding our individual disappointment and frustration, we became somewhat isolated from each other. That's how it appears in hindsight.

It seemed like a poisonous boil had been festering under the surface, and one evening in May, it finally came to a very ugly head. We'd gone for an evening walk on the cliffs. I remember the profusion of wild flowers among the silvery outcrops, and I remember thinking that for the moment we were okay – happy, even. On the way home we dropped in on some friends of David's for a quick drink. I wish we had been sensible and gone home, but hours later we were still there.

David, aided by alcohol, started venting a despair that I hadn't really understood was troubling him quite so deeply. In front of his friends, he began to direct his rant at me – perhaps because I had slipped into a despondent and rather pathetic state, focussing on what I saw as the hopelessness of our situation, about which he felt responsible and powerless. It was humiliating. He was shouting, saying things that I had never heard him say before; he was angry that I was in a distressed state and concluded that I must be mentally deranged. He repeated this assertion several times. Were these his real, unguarded feelings about me, or was it just the drink talking? It's hard to know. I couldn't help him or stop him, and I couldn't listen to him any more. The evening ended with me leaving him to grapple with whatever demons had appeared for him. The next day David did not appear, so I cancelled our planned roast dinner with his family and left our home, taking with me the expensive leg of lamb we'd bought. It was a nightmarish weekend, though the lamb was good. After spending some time with friends, I came to realise I had been unhappy for a while, and so had David. It seemed we had come to the end of the road.

Two friends surprised me by their response to our split. One warned that we should not give up on what he saw as a very strong, loving relationship, and urged us to work through this difficulty. The other, a dear old friend, counselled caution, advising against the burning of bridges. She suggested we make a commitment to each other before I left on my travels and allow some time and space to come between us, with a view to reassessing the situation later. We took all this advice seriously and did exactly what my old friend had suggested. When I left Wales some months later, it was unclear whether we would remain together, but the door was not closed.

Once I had got used to the idea that I was going it alone, something had arisen in me that made it seem ludicrous that it could be any other way. After a couple of weeks on the road, I found my own rhythm and a sense of self-sufficiency I had not really experienced before. Yet during our Skype conversation I felt a familiar frustration come alive again. David talked about all the work that he had to get through; he seemed stressed, which I understood, but he was so distant – almost cold. I wondered what, if anything, was holding us together, and what was so attractive back home? I knew it wasn't the weather. Like me, David had been happy to be alone for a while. Maybe he had realised he liked it better than being with me. I guess I wanted him to stop making excuses and just tell me the truth: that he was happier without me and didn't want to visit me. Did I want him to? I wasn't sure. It was all so tangled up.

Sitting on the sunny terrace in the late afternoon sun, surrounded by flowers and serenaded by birdsong, I felt strong within myself despite my disappointment. My feelings didn't swallow me up – this was progress. Meanwhile, Felipe had not turned up and I had still not heard from him. I was relieved – I needed time alone to allow things to settle.

*

I wake in the dark in a state of mild panic, thinking about yesterday's conversation with David. Am I anxious, angry, or both? I reflect on yesterday evening when I talked with my Swedish friends about my feelings, and was given this to think about: what if I totally accepted David as he is and didn't try to sway him or change him? What would that mean for me? It was a perceptive question. Do I want him to be different from how he is? I guess I have done. I have to admit that letting him be and accepting that he might not want to visit would mean I would have to rely more on my own resources – not look to him for security, validation or love. I am afraid that without my directions, he might make a decision that would be painful for me, but more than that, it would signify the end of our relationship, whose survival is hanging in the balance anyway. I don't think I am ready for that degree of finality. Even though I am not sure what I want, knowing that we are committed to each other, loving one another from afar, gives me a sense of security.

Actually, I am doing just fine on my own, but I can see that the notion 'I am loved' is important. What does it mean to be loved from afar? It's an idea, a comforting thought, but does love really get transmitted through the air, like radio waves, or Wi-Fi? Does it travel across space? Thoughts are so powerful that I can feel loved or unloved, and therefore happy or unhappy. 'I am loved' is a thought that I have when I believe that someone loves me, and I have a sense of wellbeing that comes from that. But actually, 'I *am* love' is also a thought, or belief, that depends on nobody else at all. What would happen if I believed that?

I make a pot of tea and sit for a while. Things start to become clear. I realise that I can be free. I can relinquish all responsibility and let David get on with his own life. Why had I thought it was my job to guide him and try to save our relationship, anyway? I have to let go of my attachment to the outcome and have faith that I will be all right, whatever might happen. I know for certain that I only want him to come if he truly, freely chooses that himself. I'm not going to give him any clues to help him decide. I feel calm again.

Having given myself all this space and the challenge to face my fear of striking out on my own, my perspective has changed. I find it easier to see the bigger picture. I want to throw everything to the wind and see how it settles. What is there to lose? I cannot lose security, because I have that here within myself – I have proved that – and what I have to gain is strength and clarity. I am ready to face the truth – there's nothing to fear. What stands in the way of this open-handed, open-hearted attitude is my anxiety about the future – a future that does not exist but is a projection into an imagined reality. If I stay here in this moment, everything is fine. So stay here, I will.

The experience I am having on this roadtrip could be seen as temporary and unreal because it seems like a holiday from my normal life. But that is not true. This is reality – *this* is real – and the rest is imagined. I left my job and my home with no agenda – no plan to pick it up again later. My old job is now filled by someone else, and my home turned out to be a short-term situation that has also been taken over by another. In fact, isn't everything temporary? It might last a long time, but it's never permanent. Suddenly I feel elated, released, present.

*

It was a wrench to leave the safe little bubble of the campsite. Everyone had become familiar during the time I was there, never leaving the confines of the site except to take a walk around the neighbouring forest or go to the nearby shop. I hadn't driven my van for two weeks, and now, getting back on the road seemed slightly daunting. However, I climbed in and started her up.

After lunch in Porto Covo, I drove to Odeceixe. There was a campsite which was open but deserted, and five miles from the village. There were no views and the amenities were closed for the winter. I decided against it, though it was getting late. I was told there was another campsite a few miles north, so I tried that, but it was the same story. It seemed pointless paying for a campsite where I would be the only camper.

I decided to take a look at the nearby beach and wound down a long steep hill. In the car park were two campervans. One was a blue and white Talbot with British plates. I cheerily said hello to the woman standing in the doorway, who looked about my age, but got little more than a grunt in reply. Her male companion smiled weakly. The other van, an aged red Renault, was occupied by an amiable young French couple who invited me to join in with their game, in which we aimed wooden blocks at circles drawn in the gravel. It was a strange variation on *boules*, and I finished in third place (apparently) though I found the scoring system unfathomable. We shared wine and stories and I went to bed feeling very positive about my first experience of free camping. I wanted to tell David I was safe, but there was no mobile signal, so I was forced to let it go. Being unable to contact him is not a bad thing at the moment. David and I are in such different places: I am on the road, having an adventure in the sun, while he remains in his world, which consists mostly of work and bad weather. During the night, a vehicle arrived and noisily manoeuvred around the car park. I woke with a start, but after a few moments of worrying about who was arriving in the small hours, and wondering if I was safe, I drifted back to sleep.

Next morning, I discovered my new neighbours were three young travellers in a bright green German van, which had been home-converted into a camper. I've seen more hand-made campers like that in Portugal than in France, where shiny, white, factory-fitted motorhomes are more the norm. The two German men and Portuguese woman travelling in the green van were students on a short trip from Lisbon. We chatted and drank coffee in the warm November sun, looking out across the empty beach as it gradually disappeared under the jade tide with its bright white breakers. They told me of a wonderful restaurant they had eaten at the night before in a tiny fishing village, just a few miles away. I must go there, they told me. The woman touched my arm several times while she talked enthusiastically about wild beaches and places where I could camp for free along the west coast, which she urged me to visit. I've noticed that Portuguese people seem to be very tactile. Often a waiter or stranger will gently grasp my arm whilst talking. Maybe I look unsteady! It feels friendly, though. I felt such warmth from this young woman as she scribbled a map for me, and I was touched that it mattered to her that I enjoyed my time in this fabulous part of her country. Sadly, my new acquaintances had to leave then, but the information would be useful. People come and go and it's easy to get talking, have a meaningful moment, let it go and move on. It's not about holding on – more about being in the flow. But it might have been fun to stow away in that bright green home-spun camper and have an adventure with this happy trio.

After waving them goodbye, I had a wonderful swim in the surf: my first sea-swim since I was with my Welsh friends. The sea was quite wild, yet clear and not too cold. I dried off in the sun and sat down to a moment of quiet contemplation in my fold-up chair next to Myfanwy. After a few blissful minutes, a man I guessed to be in his sixties approached. I hadn't noticed him before, and, continuing in the spirit of free camping friendliness that had been so easy and enjoyable that morning, I greeted him with a smile. He came and leant on the fence near to me, not bothering with a greeting, but instead carrying on as if we had been in the middle of a conversation and had already established that our worldviews were in concord. He wanted me to listen to his tale of woe, all about how terrible it was that, back home in Holland, he was forced, through taxation, to share his considerable wealth with people less fortunate than himself. 'It is my money,' he said, 'and it is my country.'

Particularly irksome to him were immigrants from war-torn Syria. It simply didn't seem fair to him that the rich should have to fork out for the poor. What he said struck me as ridiculous. Here we were in this wonderful country, enjoying the natural world and more freedom than many people dream of. There's a generosity of spirit that grows from that – at least, there is for me. I asked him what he would do if he found himself in a position similar to the refugees he was complaining about. Wouldn't he want to get to a safer place and protect his family, just like them? After all, he was free to spend his winter in sunny Portugal, escaping, like me, the gloomy weather of northern Europe. Can we imagine a life in which that was not possible? I found myself feeling simply grateful, so very grateful that I was in my shoes, not anyone else's (and particularly his). All that wealth, and he was so miserable! My question seemed not to touch him and he continued his point, but I really didn't have the inclination to listen to him. So I fixed my eyes on a bird sitting on a low bush just behind him.

'Look!' I said, 'a pretty little bird!' He looked disappointed and bemused, and just walked away. That easy!

*

This morning was perfection. I packed up and drove away from my first free camping spot, passing the couple in the Talbot van, whom I had not noticed or thought about whilst I had been busy falling in love with this magical place: the beach, the cliffs, even the gravelly car park, the green-van-people and the French couple. I drove up the hill, and after stocking up at a supermarket, I visited a wild and beautiful beach a few miles away. There were a few people about: families, sunbathers, surfers out in the distant swell, and a young couple with surfboards and wetsuits doing warm-up exercises on the sand. The waves were magnificent, and I spent a long time standing in the shallow tide just feeling them (very powerful) and watching to see if it was safe (I thought so).

I hurry up to the car park and get my board from the van. It's a cartoon-covered child's boogie board, but I don't care. I run past the proper-looking surfy couple, who are still stretching their limbs, and straight into the sea. I start wading out. This is a strange beach; it gets a little deeper and then shallower. I am quite a way out but only up to my knees. Now to my ankles again! A little further and I am thigh-deep. It feels safe, even though the waves are coming from both sides, crisscrossing wildly. It's like a big jacuzzi. The waves are fast, good for boogie-boarding, and I get whooshed along, shrieking and grinning like an idiot, like a child. Yes, I feel like a child, and I don't care what anyone thinks. Nobody knows me, and if they did, I would still not care. Out I go, time after time, to catch a suitable wave. The surfy couple are in the water, now further out than me, waiting with all the other real surfers for a proper wave on which to glide.

I am getting thrown about by the interweaving waves as I come in at speed towards the beach. It's extremely difficult to make a dignified exit from the water when you are upside-down, being scraped along the sand and rolled around like a pair of trainers in a washing machine! I hardly dare look down to see how my costume has been redistributed. I have been sand-blasted, salt-scrubbed and stone-washed. The surfy pair are still waiting for their first ride.

While I was gliding along on the fabulous wild ocean, I thought how great it would feel to be sharing these moments with someone:, a friend, my kids, someone to shriek and laugh with. But it's a bit like going to the cinema: it's not really a sociable activity. Once it starts you can't be chatting, can't make eye contact. You can only hang on to the board, being in the moment, experiencing it, and maybe talk about it afterwards.

Later, feeling intensely refreshed and alive and somewhat battered, I went in search of the restaurant that had been recommended by the lovely Portuguese woman. I found myself in a tiny fishing village – no shops or bars, just one restaurant, specialising in… fish! I decided to take myself out to dinner. After booking a table I parked up on the little road overlooking the sea, and met a Belgian couple in one of those ubiquitous white campervans. It was very modern and smart, dwarfing little Myfanwy and making her look extremely humble in contrast. They told me they had noticed me several times along the way and had got to the stage of giving me a cheery wave, but I had never responded. They guessed correctly that I didn't recognise them because their van was ordinary, like all the others, whereas my ancient van was fascinating to them. They insisted I come round for a drink after my dinner.

At seven, I went to the restaurant to take my table for one. The restaurant was crowded with couples and families, and there I was, eating alone. I felt fine and, oddly, not at all lonesome. I kept finding myself smiling and chuckling. Everything seemed rather amusing. I must have looked slightly mad, sitting alone and quietly laughing to myself. I was brought a sample of octopus salad to try, which was really a meal in itself along with the bread, fish pates and cheese – an appetiser that comes as standard in Portuguese restaurants. Obviously a few glasses of Vinho Verde were needed, for the sake of authenticity. Everything was so perfect and delicious that I couldn't help grinning. For the first time ever, I was enjoying being complete and alone at the same time. The couple on the next table were having a disagreement and looking daggers at each other. This I seemed to find very funny indeed, and, pretending not to notice them, I stared out of the window, straight ahead at my reflection, stifling further laughter. What was happening? What was this feeling? It was like being in love – a feeling of deep joy that wants to burst out; a deep sense of well-being that makes you feel generous towards all humankind. I felt I was seeing life from a new perspective, with a greater tolerance and benevolence. I felt high but sober, and completely complete.

The next course arrived. I had asked for just one small sea

bream and here were two, expertly grilled and accompanied by perfect vegetables and the best sautéed potatoes I have ever had. Portuguese chips are nearly always fantastic, in my experience. I took things very slowly and managed to eat just about everything. Of course, there's always room for ice cream and coffee. Afterwards, I thought of how I would love to go there again with David, who I knew would love it too. But David's visit was by no means certain.

I strolled along to the Belgians' swanky camper and was welcomed warmly. They were delighted to show me around their impressive motorhome, which was even more palatial inside: two flat-screen TVs, white leather upholstery, a freezer, gold taps, possibly a burglar alarm, and anything else you can think of that might belong in such a posh mobile mansion. No jacuzzi, though, which was a bit of a letdown.

Of course, they wanted to know all about Myfanwy, too. How did I manage? Did I feel safe? Did I have a toilet? I didn't tell them I had a flushing *guzunder*, though I do, and wouldn't want to be without it. There seems to be a genuine mutual respect and camaraderie among the campervan fraternity, regardless of the van's size, state or value. Being on the road is a great leveller and we all look out for one another. I immediately forgot the names of the Belgian couple, possibly as a result of drinking quite a lot of wine with dinner, but I found them to be kindly people. As the evening got late, talking became tiring, partly because we were using our inadequate bits of each other's language and partly because I seem to love peace and quiet more than anything these days. So I retreated to my cosy little home on wheels, and slept like a log.

*

It's hard for me to stay still and drop the notion that I ought to be somewhere, finding the next place where I will rest for a while: the special place I dreamed about back in Wales. I imagined a village: a dusty street with donkeys and tiny old ladies, dressed in black, ambling past in the noonday heat while I looked on from a shady porch. There would be palm trees and the sea not far away – nothing much going on.

I am exploring the wild southwest corner of Portugal, taking in places that Felipe had suggested I visit. It seems so long ago that we were toiling under the baking sun together. I messaged him recently, and he replied that he had tried to contact me to say he was coming for lunch when I was at the campsite. That was when my phone and the internet were down, so his message had vanished into nowhere. It could be simply that our limited knowledge of one another's language is open to misinterpretation, but I get the feeling he has taken offence. Does he think I was avoiding him, playing games? Or is he playing games? Or neither? Those few days with no connection to the outside world might have been rather significant. I wonder what would have happened if he had come to visit at that time when I was doubting David's intentions, and I am relieved that the moment has passed. Perhaps someone was looking after me by disabling the satellite. I'd wanted nothing more than friendly company, but what did Felipe think I wanted? And what did *he* want? I also wonder where my Swedish friends have ended up and whether I will see them again. They were heading down to the Algarve to find somewhere to stay for a month or so. I will call them. But first, I think, a walk is in order – or a swim, or a wash in the river. There's no rush.

In the afternoon, I wove slowly south along the coast road,

stopping for lunch and a walk at another wild and exquisite beach of silver-gold sand and interweaving waves. There was a huge car park, and when I arrived there were quite a few campervans; but returning after my walk, I saw that everyone was leaving. The sun was low in the sky and I wanted to park up for the night, but I had become indecisive. I didn't feel right about being the only camper van in this large, exposed space. I guess I have developed a sort of instinct about free camping. It has to feel right; I have to feel safe. I was sad to leave, but I knew this was not the place for me to stay alone for the night. I consulted Tanya and found that I was only an hour or so away from Sagres.

I arrived at nightfall, feeling bit desperate to get settled for the night. Turning in to the road for the campsite, I spotted four familiar figures: it was the Swedish angels with their two little dogs! What are the chances? After helping me find a good spot where my solar panel would not be damaged by falling pine cones the size of small melons, they invited me for drinks, and a few Drambuies loosened my tongue. I was so excited to see them again.

*

The sun is peeping through the morning clouds on the horizon. I see my new surroundings for the first time in daylight and I like the look of this campsite in Sagres, with its tall pine trees and hedged plots. It feels relaxed and friendly. I go to reception to use the Wi-Fi, and there is an email from David saying he is flying out in a few weeks, all being well. Delight, relief and uncertainty collide in quite a pleasant way. Did I really doubt him? Did I really let go completely of my attachment to the idea of him coming to see me? He wants to start afresh after the communication that went so horribly wrong. We both want that now. Today seems even more beautiful.

*

I have spent a lot of time with my Swedish friends, whom I find quite fascinating and stimulating company. Ivan lived as a Zen monk for several years and retains something of a cool, Zen outlook on life, as well as a very dry sense of humour. He stands back from drama and always seems relaxed, even when he is playing agent provocateur, which I think he enjoys. Maira is warm, very talkative, empathetic and expressive. The three of us have spirited conversations which I enjoy. They seem to view life from almost opposing philosophical standpoints. When I mention this, Ivan just smiles and says, 'Opposites attract.' It certainly seems that they love each other very much.

One afternoon, Maira looked upset and showed me a pamphlet about a charity helping stray dogs in a faraway country.

'Look at these poor animals,' she said. 'These cats and dogs are living in the streets – starving, dying. It's terrible! When we go home I want to adopt another dog. Why don't you take one, too? If all our friends did that, the problem would be solved: just one dog for each family!'

I didn't know where to start, having had no plans to take on such a responsibility – actually, having no plans about my future at all. Ivan chipped in, asking, 'How do you know they are starving? How do you even know they exist? How do you know the whole world exists if you're not there to see it?'

'Because I know!' Maira protested. 'Don't start with all that cold Zen stuff. I care about these animals. It's really upsetting.'

'So who is suffering?' Good question, I thought to myself.

'It is called empathy, Ivan,' Maira retorted, with a slightly exasperated huff. Good point, I thought, again not saying it out loud, wondering if we'd ever reach a point of harmony and enjoy a quiet moment.

*

Yesterday, Ivan and Maira invited me to a concert of sacred songs at a centre for spirituality and yoga along the coast. I accepted, of course. In fact, it turned out to be more of a sing-song than a performance. We all joined in with long, meditative *bhajans* – devotional songs – and by the end of it, the small circle of mostly strangers felt more like a group of old friends, though very few words had passed between us. I can't put my finger on it, but something happened during the chanting – a change in vibration, perhaps – and I felt serene afterwards. The whole group went out for lunch together, which was thoroughly joyful.

Today, I woke early at the beautiful beach where we had parked our campervans for the night after the *bhajan* singing. I went to sit on the dunes to look at the sea and be alone. Maira and Ivan are entertaining, conscious, creative people and it's wonderful to hang out with them, yet I fear they are driving me slightly mad. Is it them or is it just me? I can't tell any more. Again and again they do their dance of the heart and the mind – non-attachment versus attachment. There's a lot of talking. When Maira gets into her passionate stride on an issue, Ivan throws in a Zen *koan* like a handgrenade, which drives Maira crazy. I guess that's the point of *koans* – and I do love *koans* – to confuse the mind. Just when it looks as though

74

Maira is about to explode with rage, she suddenly bursts out laughing, and then Ivan joins in. It is impossible for me to keep a straight face – it's two against one – and it feels wonderful to laugh.

I wonder if they enjoy the drama of it all. I just have to roll with it, and, anyway, I suspect that their little flare-ups are only reflections of myself. I recognise I can get caught up in taking a stand on an issue, yet there's a part of me that is quiet and mildly amused, that sits back and watches. I like the quiet part, and right now, it seems to be prevailing. It's as though I have been rewired and the old wiring still has some juice in it. The interplay between these two different modes boggles my brain sometimes. I suspect it has already boggled theirs. Or, perhaps, as a couple, they are an actual walking, talking *koan*! Their purpose in life is to befuddle my rational mind and release me from the illusion that anything makes sense. Though I have come to love them, I have to get away for a while, be quiet and find my own balance.

*

I left my friends and went off along the coast, driving from place to place, and gave myself a task, which was to find beautiful beaches and free camping spots where David and I might camp when he arrives in a week or so. It has rained a little almost every day and it's colder now, so it's more difficult to be outside and mix with people or just enjoy the great outdoors. The days feel shorter since the clocks went back. The dark evenings are long and potentially lonesome: just me and my van. The strange thing is that I don't feel lonely.

My purpose was to reach Portugal. Now that I am here, I

have no destination, and I could even say I am pointless – direction-less. Yet I have hit a seam of self-containment, maybe even contentment. Alone for a great deal of the time, I find myself quite fulfilled just by meeting the everyday needs of being alive. I get up, have tea – slowly coming into full alertness – and put my bed away; I go somewhere new to check it out, or stay put and potter about; I go off on my bicycle, or walk, or swim; I shop for basic foods; I read, I write; I go to bed early. I am awake at three till five most mornings. During that time I stretch, relax, contemplate. Time passes.

Much as I love a bit of social contact, I find that interacting with people is exhausting. There must be something in me that becomes unbalanced when I am with people. I guess it has something to do with the engagement of our minds. It takes a lot of energy to be in the realm of thoughts and opinions. I think this is all part of the rewiring that's going on. It's surprising how much space and quiet I need. In solitude, I find peace, and for the first time in my life I am not afraid of the space. It's not empty or boring, but full and satisfying. This is quite a revelation. I feel complete, and at the same time I am looking forward to David's company, knowing I can relax with him. Being joined by him will give me someone to dine with, walk and talk with – someone to play with. I don't feel needy; it's more that I want us to share this space together. I would love for him to find joy, too. I wonder what it will be like to be together after these months alone. I don't need to think about what happens after he goes back. I don't want to focus on it. After all, it's just an idea – a thought.

Having found neutral gear, I don't feel the need to think much about anything. I am vacant. Am I losing touch, sliding into a sort of void? Perhaps I've been in some kind of deep, unfathomable process, too embryonic to describe coherently. My mind appears empty, yet there's something lurking in the depths beyond my everyday consciousness. Writing is a magical process, and though it seems I am merely noting down small events, or exploring modest ideas that come to me, something else is disturbed. I notice a crack – a previously hidden doorway. The prospect of entering it and exploring a subterranean world is daunting. Like contemplating untangling a tightly knotted ball of string, it's tempting to discard the idea and throw the string in the bin; but perhaps that's a bit lazy. Will the passage from the hidden door lead to anything worth the effort of excavating?

In truth, worse than the fear that there may be no treasure hidden beneath the surface is the suspicion that what I will find there in the depths will be exceptionally banal: merely stuff that everyone else already knows, even though it seems profound to me. But maybe that is the point. I am not climbing Everest, or crossing a desert on a camel. I know mine is not an epic journey – but it's life-changing all the same. Something is happening to me, and I need to honour that. I need to honour my journey.

*

I have been trying to escape from something – I mean always. I look back again at that time when I had a breakdown (though I prefer the term 'breakthrough', or simply 'break', suggested by a friend who survived one; it always makes me smile, because there's a deep truth in those labels) and I realise I was not well attuned to the world I lived in. I felt unable to cope with the barrage of feelings, demands and crises that came at me repeatedly, which sometimes felt like gunfire. Things that other people seemed to manage effortlessly completely flattened me.

A breakdown can be seen as a distinct event, a random depressive episode: possibly the result of something going wrong with the synapses and a lack of serotonin. At the time, I knew what had brought it on – or at least I thought I did. But now I start to connect the dots and follow the thread back into the deeper past. Before I broke down (which makes me think of rusty, clapped out car holding up the traffic) I had been busy working and bringing up a family, just living a fairly unremarkable life and doing *normal* things, but I was often in survival mode. I was stressed a lot of the time and, frankly, teetering on the edge of total collapse. I know I am not alone in finding life stressful; such is the modern world, it seems.

During that time, I was slowly regaining equilibrium after a long period of grief for my brother, who had died. He was the younger of my two older brothers, and a complex person: a sensitive, somewhat troubled child; a wild and rebellious teenager; an adult who was flamboyant, creative and vulnerable to glowering, depressive moods. As a child growing up, I looked up to him and saw him as a glamorous hero. I followed him around, as little siblings do, and tried to impress him and emulate him, the results of which were often inappropriate for a young girl. I am not sure if I really understood myself to be a person separate from him until I was in my early twenties. During my teenage years, when our parents were going through their divorce, we became very close and, for the first time ever, we both chose to spend a lot of time together. For a while my brother became my friend, my ally and, to an extent, my equal. Twenty years later, he became sick. His illness and death were devastating, needless to say.

And even before those harrowing, terrible years, I had found myself, periodically, in a state of confusion and turmoil. I felt like a small boat on an eternally stormy sea, desperately trying to keep myself afloat. It was as if I had been startled on arrival in this world and then continued to find everything a little bewildering, and I hadn't been given the necessary tools or armour to deal with life. I didn't much like the person I found myself to be, but who else could I be? What else could I be? I tried a lot of things – some edifying, some helpful, others destructive. I was searching for a path that would lead me away from the discontent I felt.

Being alone was something to avoid. I believed myself to be an extrovert, someone who thrived on constant company and activity. I have no idea where that notion came from, and I question it now. Actually, my happiest memories of childhood involved being immersed in both nature and solitude. Somehow, though, over time, I lost the thread – my connection to myself, to my *being*. My mind became a very busy place.

By my forties, I was exhausted from trying to make sense of my life by analysing what felt like a catalogue of things that had gone wrong, and brooding about all the things that had hurt me. I was trying to force it into some sort of order that would make it make sense. Perhaps that's what killed off my serotonin, zapped my synapses and made me hold up the traffic.

Now, at last, the past doesn't hurt so much. I can stop running. I am no longer afraid it will catch me up and devour me. I can face it squarely. Looking from where I am now, miraculously, I find that the pain of the past has dispersed, exposing solid ground.

*

I am sitting in the passenger seat, looking out at the sea. Surfers arrive in vans to assess the waves. I think that today they'll be disappointed. It rained heavily this morning, but now the sun keeps peeping through the clouds and then, suddenly, it's very hot. I am an imposter. I have a little van just like theirs, and a spot in this small beachside parking area where young people park up for the night, hoping for early morning surf, but I am a middle-aged woman who doesn't do real surfing. From a distance I might possibly be mistaken for a surfer girl in this context. Amazing but true: I still get wolf-whistles, especially when riding my bike with my bare legs on show and my untameable curly hair flowing out behind me. If the whistler got closer he would soon realise I am his mother's age. Strangely, though, I find this subculture the most accepting and friendly group on the road. They don't seem concerned with age, gender or anything – only waves.

Talking of mothers: an interesting thing happened between Maira and me yesterday when I'd returned for another stay at the campsite. She is not old enough to be my mum, but something has been emerging in me lately and I guess some old, buried mother/daughter stuff got triggered. It was reminiscent of when I was a teenager. Sometimes I wanted to be quiet and not have to think. I might have seemed a bit sullen. It wasn't pleasant for my mother, who was having her own tribulations at the time. I remember clearly the sudden flaring up of a row that I am sure neither of us wanted to have. It seemed to come from nowhere and escalate from nothing to a full-force battle in seconds. It was one of many similar conflicts. I see now that I had no skills with which to assert my need for peace and solitude. I had no power. Mum wanted a polite 'good morning' and a chat before school, but my reality in those days seemed dark, complex and confusing. Mornings were particularly painful, so cheerful conversation was beyond my capabilities. How could she know what I was experiencing when I was never able to explain it to her, or even to myself?

In my youth I had always felt my mum had neglected me, and had little time for my needs. It was only after my brother's death that she and I began to build a good relationship. Following our shared bereavement, things changed and she wanted to make things right between us. She was regretful, acknowledging that she had been preoccupied when I was a child, trying to mend her own life, and she had not truly valued me. Over time we talked and got to know one another anew. Our relationship became stronger, more supportive and loving.

Yesterday life threw me an opportunity to assert my needs: not to dominate or be unkind, but just to say what I needed. For a moment Maira unknowingly played my mum and I was the teenager, wanting to remain undisturbed in my silent, peaceful bubble. She came over to my van during my morning meditation. What she said is not important – she did nothing wrong; she just wanted to engage on some subject, and I didn't. I became frozen and my mind went blank; I couldn't find the words to speak clearly and simply, so I listened for a while, getting irritated, then I waffled and tried to evade conversation. I must have blurted out something about needing space, but what I actually said was probably confusing and mildly hostile. Instead of getting back to my peace and quiet, I spent a long time with Maira trying to undo what had turned into a tangled, awkward knot.

I had been just as inept as my teenage self. What did I think might be the consequence of speaking honestly? What was I so scared of? Was Maira going to bite me? Was my mother going to reject me? Did I think friendship and love were so flimsy that I could lose them by voicing a modest need? It's not personal, and it's not about Maira, or my mum. If it's about anyone, it's about me and how I attempt to project some image of myself as pleasant and compliant. It's a cover-up that I suppose fools almost no one. Perhaps I have always been afraid of people. I am sure there's a reason why this little clash happened at a time when I have been preoccupied with untangling threads from the past. It was an opportunity to reassess things.

*

After yesterday's afternoon of sunshine we are being treated to more rain. It feels just like home. Today I met a woman of my age: a solo traveller, like me. I realise I have met only two lone women on the whole trip so far, and the other was just leaving a place as I was arriving. Campervanners usually come in pairs, sometimes even with matching his 'n' hers walking clothes, like tiny teams.

Adele and I talked, drank coffee and swam together. It was really wonderful to spend time with a fellow female traveller. She had a lot to say, perhaps because, like me, she hadn't had much opportunity for female conversation. We skipped peripheral issues and got straight into the pithy stuff, give or take the odd observation about the weather. I found myself enjoying being in the role of listener more than talker – a relatively new position for me and my chatterbox mind. It was relaxing just sitting back and absorbing her words rather than rummaging for stories I might have to offer. Adele was very open and seemed to trust me with her concerns of the heart. It felt like an honour to be taken into her confidence.

I gave Adele my book by Eckhart Tolle, which I had read in the spring and now felt I had absorbed thoroughly enough to let it go. If that turns out to be a delusion I can buy another copy. I had first picked it up at a friend's house several years earlier, flicked through and thought that I had understood the message. Years later it fell into my hands again and I read it very slowly, over several weeks. This time I didn't understand it with my mind; instead, what Tolle was talking about dropped into another place, a place that was now more receptive and fertile – the ground already prepared. I *experienced* what Tolle was showing me: that what I am is something other than my mind. I started to notice how my mind distracts me with its thoughts and that there was a *me* that could be distracted – or, ideally, that could remain undisturbed and steady. Underneath the clutter of the mind was clarity, stillness and peace. I didn't instantly find myself rooted in a state of constant bliss; nevertheless, there had been a shift, and life was better for that shift. It was work in progress.

*

I've noticed that some people appear disturbed when they discover that I am travelling alone. The French campervanners I meet along the way invariably exclaim:

'You are alone? But where is your 'usband?' At first I simply answered that I was on a solo journey, and they seemed to find this surprising and alarming.

'But are you not afraid?'

'No!' I told them. Well, I wasn't afraid until they mentioned it! There was an occasion in Sagres, at the campsite, when two middle-aged French men in a very smart Winnebago, after gleaning that I was on my own, started laughing and shouting, suggesting I join them as they were free of their wives.

'We could all have a good time together, no?' they called from their plot. That is when I started to change my story a little:

'Yes, I am alone; my husband had to go back to Wales, but he's joining me in a few days.' Is it strange that, in this century, women travelling alone are still seen as an anomaly, a bit loose or irresponsible, or perhaps something to be pitied?

'Poor girl, she has no husband!', or, 'She must be running from something.' Is that what they are thinking?

A few years before my trip, David and I went to a tiny music festival in the mountains in mid-Wales, and there we watched as a sizeable truck came across the camping field and pulled in next to us. Out climbed a diminutive woman, who glanced at us as we watched her put wedges under the chunky wheels. It was hard not to stare. She looked so small against the vehicle, which had been converted into a quirky home on wheels. We got talking and she told us of her travels. She spent part of each year driving through Spain to Morocco, alone, in her fairly eccentric-looking rig. She was nearly seventy, and I remember thinking, 'Wow, that's brave. I could never do that.' I warmed to her and enjoyed her stories, some of which I suspected contained a little exaggeration when she described scary things that had happened or had almost happened to her. Still, perhaps I didn't want to hear about what could go wrong for a lone woman going on such an adventure, even though I had no intention, at that time, of doing any such thing. I didn't want to believe that there was anything bad out there to spoil the lovely picture that was emerging in my mind of travel, freedom and independence.

Adele was about to leave for the next leg of her journey, and

I realised it was time for me to leave too and find somewhere close to Faro to spend the night. Tomorrow I'd collect David from the airport, two months after he waved goodbye to me at the start of this trip. I am very keen to see him, and I now know that it's not just so that I have a dinner buddy and playmate, but because I need to see *him*, David, and find out what exists between us. We have had a difficult year and have both said that things needed to change. I am unsure about him, and about where we are going. Yet now I am excited, and I can't wait to give him a massive hug. This will be a journey for him too.

After a two-hour drive in pouring rain and heavy evening traffic, I arrive at the *aire* in Estoi, twenty minutes from Faro airport, and I walk into the only cafe I find open. I am now completely comfortable entering a strange place, being the focus of curious attention and throwing myself on the kindness and tolerance of strangers whose language I barely speak. I am no longer self-conscious; it doesn't matter. In this place I am the only female, apart from the waitress/bartender, who welcomes me sweetly. I use sign language and, this time, Google Translate, and manage to understand the menu from the pictures on my tiny screen. I order the *prata do dia,* which today is a casserole with rice. It's delicious, as is the wine which comes with the deal – as much as I like. The bread goes into my bag for breakfast.

All the way west to east along the N125, the Algarve's main road, I saw dozens of stands piled up with oranges and clementines. I wanted to buy some, but the conditions were difficult for stopping. I kept hoping for the perfect lay-by where I could pull in and buy a huge net of fruit for a few pennies, but it never appeared.

Sitting at my table for one, I notice that the men at the large central table are peeling and eating clementines, which they are picking out of a bucket on the floor. I consult my phone again, brave the group and say in parrot-fashion Portuguese:

'I would like to buy some clementines, please.' I am answered in English:

'No, you can't buy them, but you can *have* them. How many?' They all laugh.

'I'd like six,' I say, and a man gives me a carrier bag full. As I am settling my very modest bill at the bar, another man comes over and insists I take another bagful! It is a great end to the evening, with lots of smiles and *'obrigada's'*. Back at the van, I count over two dozen sweet and juicy clementines. This is such a wonderful country.

I got up early and made the short trip to the airport. After a brief wait in arrivals, David appeared and we bear-hugged in front of the automatic doors. It was so good to see him. Thanks to Tanya, we took a surprising and circuitous route that snaked up into the hinterland of the Algarve. It seemed familiar and homely, and I realised this was the area near Moncarapacho, where I'd been driven around by Martin and Catherine. I thought it would be nice to show David their house, though they were no longer in residence. The lanes seemed so familiar now, but perhaps that was only because they all looked the same. We couldn't find the house, so we made our way to the coast.

The eastern Algarve has a special and distinct character, quite different from the wild west coast, and could be a different country from the built-up resort strip between Lagos and Quarteira. This area is unspoiled and a bit rundown. The hillsides are scattered with white cottages. Small terraced villas, faced in Arabic tilework, line the streets of the villages.

I had booked three nights in a small hotel overlooking the

large tidal river in Tavira. We checked in, rested and then went to Julia's restaurant, where I knew we would be well fed, having eaten there with my friends in what seemed a far distant time but was, in fact, only about six weeks ago. David and I clicked straight back into our comfortable togetherness and enjoyed a long lunch of freshly caught sea bass, a fabulous salad and wine. Julia and her family run this lovely little place, and she has a character well suited to her role of welcoming hungry customers, treating each one like an old friend.

After our lunch, Julia came and sat with us and told us about a terrible accident that had happened the previous night, just along the street from the restaurant. A Scandinavian couple had dined at her place, drunk a fair amount of wine and left late. The man had been very chatty, engaging with other diners, while his wife was silent and, according to Julia, as pale as the white tablecloth upon which our coffee cups now sat. Back at their hotel, she went on, this poor woman had climbed the steep steps and, at the top, had fallen to her death. What a horrific story! How tragic and shocking for the man to see his wife die like that. We walked to our hotel in a sober mood and went to bed, realising that the steep steps of the dreadful story were, in fact, the very steps we had just climbed to get to our room, where we now lay in the bed where this couple had spent their last ever night together. This was not the sort of thing you expect on a romantic reunion weekend, and I felt sick at the thought of what had happened.

Next morning in the breakfast room, the widowed husband was sitting talking to the other guests about the incident, and we joined in for a while. He seemed to be holding up well, but I guessed he was in shock and just trying to keep it all together while he waited for the police to come and see him later. The incident was further dissected by Julia when we revisited our now favourite restaurant for Saturday night's dinner. On Sunday we ate there one more time, and on Monday morning we checked out and drove northwest into the hills, stopping briefly at Silves.

The day was dull and overcast, but when we reached the top of mount Foia with its magnificent panoramic views, we were rewarded with a clear spell and a beautiful place to stay the night. We avoided the actual viewpoint, which is blighted by a forest of masts and ugly buildings, and instead pulled in to a nearby picnic spot with a sacred spring and view equally splendid, though technically only half as panoramic. We parked looking out beyond the Algarve to the sparkling sea, the spring gurgling and splashing right behind us and nobody else around. The clouds began to gather again on the horizon and made for a spectacular sunset.

After a while, an old VW camper van rolled up. and a young German couple came to say hello. They were students taking a year out to tour Europe. They had a bed and a single gas ring, which they used outside for cooking, and not much else. Some weeks earlier, they told us, their van had been broken into in northern Portugal, and all their belongings – even their clothes – had been stolen. We shared chocolate, beer and wine, and I gave them a collection of things I didn't really need but which I had continued to carry with me, in the hope that they would be useful to someone. This couple seemed the perfect recipients, and I hoped they would bring them good luck.

Having overindulged on chocolate and red wine, I woke up feeling rough. We drank the wonderful water from the spring, where several people came to fill their bottles during the morning. The heavy, glowering sky was a fitting accompaniment to my hangover and gloomy frame of mind. My doubts about David and our relationship were surfacing again. I couldn't say what was troubling me exactly, but I felt uneasy. Was I just happier and lighter on my own?

David and I are normally totally comfortable around each other. We rarely quarrel. He is a fairly quiet person. In fact, when I try to describe him, I find I am a bit lost. Perhaps this is because we are so familiar to one another. He is a still-waters-run-deep sort of man, sensitive and sometimes lacking in confidence, except when he drinks too much. He is also extremely talented and creates things from wood, including entire buildings, that are beautiful, simple and practical. His work is done with such efficiency that it seems to appear without effort (I know this isn't true). He is a natural, gifted. Elegance, proportion and integrity are vitally important to him. He loves his work.

He's said that he believes he was born in the wrong time and belongs to a bygone era – somewhere around the late nineteenth century, perhaps – and I share his sense of discomfort with some aspects of modern life. Are we unusual or do lots of people feel this way? When I was young, my ambition was to live as a peasant, tending a garden, growing herbs and food. That got a few laughs, but I was serious. Not that I wanted to be poor and struggling to survive under the oppression of an overlord, but I wasn't materialistic or aspirational, and I found so many man-made things desperately ugly. I wanted peace and to live as close to the earth as possible without actually being a mole or a slug. It was a deep yearning, a respect and passion for natural wisdom, beauty, simplicity and tranquillity – and yes, it may be idealistic. The world is changing so fast and there's barely time to absorb anything.

Perhaps the old wisdoms will be lost forever. David understands all of this – he feels the same. His work springs from this philosophy, and when metal screws and bolts rust, perhaps David's structures, pegged in the old fashioned way, will stay together.

Periodically David becomes disconnected from himself, from his heart. I can almost hear his mind telling him things that are not helpful, not loving, not *true* – things that are born of deep emotional wounds that still fester and hurt from time to time. When this happens I try to get him to name his feelings, to *see* them. Of course, sometimes I come up against resistance, which is entirely understandable; yet when he finally comes to observe what is going on and expresses it, he changes quickly – sometimes instantly – and it is like the sun coming out from behind a cloud. This is what I love about him: he is willing to face his 'stuff' – to look at it, expose it and let it go as best he can. He is always happy when it's done. This time, though, I felt unable to reach him. I couldn't find his heart and felt I was spending time with his mind talk, not with the loving, funny best friend I know so well. Perhaps I didn't have the energy to delve into his old stuff this time. I wanted him to stop rerunning that useless old programme. He'd have to sort it out for himself.

The rain continued over the next two days as we sheltered in Myfanwy, free camping in places with spectacular views of wild waves seen through steamed-up windows, and, beyond them, the mizzle. We drove to Odemira, where the river was racing by, high and dramatic, and the colour of strong tea, with a dash of milk. It was Wednesday, which meant that the excellent fish restaurant I had been to a few weeks before was closed, so we went to Zambujeira, where we hoped to find a good place to eat and celebrate David's birthday. Wet but optimistic, we entered the bar of what seemed a nice restaurant and saw two very intriguing-looking fellows sitting in the corner. This was to be a catalytic meeting – a turning point in so many ways.

Marco and Dominic had met in Fatima, the famous town north of Lisbon where three shepherd children are said to have seen an apparition of the Virgin Mary in 1917. A chapel was erected in honour of the vision and the town became became a place of pilgrimage. Within two years of the event, two of the three children died in the flu epidemic that had swept through Europe. I have heard that Fatima is a rather strange place.

Dominic was in his twenties and on a quest to find meaning in his life.

'I walked very slowly the Camino, from France through Spain, to Santiago de Compostela. I had many questions in me,' he told us in good English with a Czech accent.

'Did you camp in a tent?' David asked.

'At first I had big rucksack, but I saw that I don't need things. I give away all belongings and ask to stay at houses.'

'And what if there is no place for you to stay?'

'I sleep in hedge.'

He pointed to a small knapsack. 'Now I travel very light. This is all I have.'

He looked sweet, with dark, child-like eyes and a wide, open face. He was very thin from walking, living rough and surviving on whatever charity people gave him.

He had joined forces with Marco, in whose car he now travelled and slept. Marco was Belgian, older and perhaps more worldly wise than Dominic, with lines on his serious, sensitive face. His English was almost non-existent.

'How do you communicate?' I asked Marco, who looked to Dominic and prompted him to answer.

'I speak in English, which he knows only a little, and he speaks in French. I am learning a few words, but really we speak telepathy of the heart. We understand each other.'

Then Marco made a long speech which was barely fathomable, but some of it made sense.

'The world is trouble for me. Man is trouble. Religion is trouble. Priests and churches... they... trap... make prison... no freedom. All men... all peoples is free... but not no more. It make man very sick,' he said solemnly.

We spent a few hours talking with the two men, understanding as well as we could and buying rounds of hot chocolate and beer.

Suddenly Dominic said: 'We have come here to see someone called Mooji. We go there on Sunday.'

'I am going too,' I heard myself say, because it was true. At that exact moment I committed myself to going to see Mooji, a man who I had not really thought about whilst travelling but who was deeply connected with this trip to Portugal. We said our farewells after Dominic told us that if we went to the bar in a certain tiny village in the hills, we would be directed to Mooji's ashram.

A few years before my road trip, I was in the habit of trawling the internet for answers to some questions that were perplexing me at the time. I had put a question into the search engine, though I can't remember what I asked, and up came a video that introduced me to Mooji: a man whom some refer to as a Zen master. He does not call himself a guru, a philosopher nor anything else, but through his talking points people towards profound realisation. Some people get it, some don't.

There's no dogma, no affiliation with any church or cult or anything. He asks nothing of anyone, and has stirred a lot of interest in hundreds of thousands of people all over the world.

Through listening to Mooji over the years via the wonders of the internet, quite subtly, something began to change in me. I was waking up a little bit – beginning to see life differently. The discontent I'd felt in spring before I left Wales was a force that pushed me to decide to go travelling, and although I didn't consciously think I was going to Portugal because Mooji lives there, I secretly hoped that somehow I might find myself going to one of his *satsangs* – open discussions. Then time moved on; I sort of forgot about him and planned my itinerary around other things, including nothing at all. I planned to have no plan and see what life would do to guide me.

Our dinner was not good, but it didn't matter all that much. We laughed about it, partly because we have a history of duff meals on our birthdays and partly because, for me, anyway, there was something much more important going on. We spent the night free camping in a car park overlooking the beach, along with five other campervans. Next morning, a council official came and berated us all for taking up the spaces in the car park, though it would otherwise have been deserted, such was the wild, wet weather. We were about to leave anyway, and as we slowly drove away, we noticed a car that we realised must belong to Marco. We stopped to say hello, but he and Dominic were not at home. The modest, battered hatchback was covered in colourful stickers, the interior bedecked with rosaries, dreamcatchers and feathers, and the dashboard completely obscured by a host of effigies and religious iconography representing all the religions known to humankind. It was quite a sight. Marco was covering all bases and honouring all spiritual paths, but I doubt he could see the speedometer.

Later I took David to the little beach that had so enchanted me weeks before when I had first tried free camping. We sat in the van, wipers swishing, kettle singing, and watched the ferocious tide crashing onto the rocks. The drama was enhanced by occasional flashes of lightning. Gradually the rain petered out and we were blessed with a fine evening for our short drive to the fish restaurant, where we would have our faith in Portuguese cuisine restored. We celebrated David's birthday again, this time with dorado and octopus.

The next few days were spent wild camping on the coast, where we enjoyed gorgeous walks on clifftops festooned with wild flowers, and inland, where we parked next to a reservoir that looked more like a glorious natural lake than a man-made dam. On the day of our visit to Mooji, we woke early at the water's edge with a sense of happy anticipation. We heated up reservoir water for a thorough bathing and hair-washing experience. It felt good to get really clean. We drove through some exceptionally beautiful soft countryside to the village we had been told about. I walked into the bar where a few old men stood or sat enjoying a Sunday lunchtime drink, and there, in the middle of the room, sat a beautiful youngish man, who looked at me, stood up and hugged me as though we were old friends and he'd been sitting there waiting for me to arrive. I guessed he was on his way to Mooji's. He knew the way and we gave him a lift.

It had started to rain again, this time with determination, and driving up the rough track felt like navigating a small river in places. As we neared the top we were greeted and directed by smiling, radiant people. We parked, entered the building and took our seats. We sat there in silence for a long time while scores of people slowly filed in and settled down. Beautiful music drifted in the air and there was an atmosphere of serenity, mixed with expectancy. We caught a glimpse of Dominic and Marco, but they didn't seem to recognise us. Eventually in came Mooji, a dark-skinned, Buddha-like man with dreadlocks down to his waist.

Seeing Mooji in real life was wonderful. He was just as he had seemed when I'd watched him on the internet, but being there in his presence was extra special. As I sat listening to him respond to people asking their questions, I realised that the past few years have been, for me, a time of gradual awakening – a journey that started in turmoil which has gradually ebbed away, almost without my noticing. In its place have come relative harmony and clarity. Everything he said that Sunday afternoon seemed absolutely pertinent to me and confirmed so much of what I had been experiencing. I felt completely peaceful, as though I was in exactly the place I belonged. In that large beautiful room, surrounded by strangers from all over the world, I felt as though I had come home.

*

It seems that something was ignited by my so-called breakdown. The path I had been walking had come to a dead end and for a while I was truly lost, the old *me* gone. There was nothing to do but give in and surrender to the process of falling apart. My children had gone off to make their way in the world, my partner of several years had suddenly left, and I could no longer continue with the work I had been doing for the previous two decades. My home felt like a huge empty nest with only me left in it, and I was an injured, bewildered bird with a broken heart. All the things that I had held on to as proof of my identity simply shattered. I didn't know how to live any more. For about two years I was often alone, fortunately in a safe place. The only way I could get through it was to stay very still, be quiet, and take each day at a time – each moment at a time. It was a very intense and lonely experience.

Could it be that the broken pieces of my identity fell into a heap and that, after a long time resting in peace, the heap started decomposing – turning to compost? And, as it decayed, perhaps it got warm, as compost heaps do, silently smouldering until someone opened a window and a breeze blew in – just enough oxygen to feed it. Maybe a little fire started, burning away all the old stuff and blazing until there was nothing left. Perhaps, after a while, new shoots started to appear and grew up into the light, fed by the nutritious waste.

Life does not stay stagnant for long, and maybe life knew exactly what it was doing. Slowly I recovered my strength. But, importantly, I never recovered the old me – not really. I didn't try to reclaim the life, the identity I'd had before. I just kept walking. It was as though I had experienced a brush with death – the death of who I used to be – and I didn't dare look back.

My breakdown was the breaking down of the false identity I had tried so hard to maintain and to believe in. It *was* a death – the death of the illusion of all that was not truly me: all the memories, conditioning, experiences and projections that had come together to form what I thought of as *myself*. It was not as scary as it might sound, to lose this constructed identity. Once I let go – and I had very little choice but to let go – everything gradually got better and better. I discovered that there was something that existed beyond the *construct*, something that would endure. I was no longer hostage to threats to my identity.

This is how I now see my breakdown. And I know that this road trip is part of that same journey. I was desperate for solitude, and I think that is because I needed to consolidate the change that has been happening and put it to the test. It is an ongoing process – acclimatising to myself, getting accustomed to experiencing my life in the present. I can see all this from where I am now – the place that Mooji points to. When I was in the thick of it I could not see. I was like a little mouse scurrying around a maze. I didn't know where I was.

After sitting with Mooji I knew, not with my mind but in my heart, that I could relax, let go. My experience now made sense to me – it had been explained and validated. I was free of any doubt. Now, rather than trying to *live* my life and *manage* everything, I could trust life. I could let life live through me.

*

Before I left Wales, a close friend reminded me that wherever I go, I will take myself and my baggage with me. It is true – I can never be apart from myself. So what about the baggage? The baggage came along with me, of course. But through spending time in solitude I did a lot less talking, interacting. Having less to feed on, my mind quietened down a little. It didn't crowd me out when it started its routine of chatter.

*

I see the baggage carousel go round and round. There's the battered old suitcase case full of memories; the heavy backpack stuffed with worries; the projector that so often throws frightening images up onto the screen; and so on. Can I simply let it continue without me? Who is *me*? Who watches the carousel? Is it my mind watching my mind? This was the same conundrum that kept me busy from time to time during my childhood. Can I locate the place I am watching from? Is it a place? Or is it a state?

Anyway, the baggage will still be there if it's needed – picking it up again is not difficult, but it's not attractive, either. It is habit, conditioning, that makes me want to reclaim it – or, perhaps more accurately, let it reclaim me. If I want any peace, I have to form a new habit, a discipline: watching, witnessing the baggage carousel, letting it go by. I have to practise being in this witness state, remind myself to do it. A few minutes spent quietly enjoying a cup of tea might sound like a joke – 'Start the day with a cuppa and really wake up!' – but the making and drinking of tea is a little ritual: my way of stopping and letting everything be. My tea ceremony is my practice. And now I notice that it's not even dependent on tea.

*

Something else happened during our afternoon at Mooji's. David had been unsure about joining me at the *satsang*, but in the end, he decided to come along. We were sitting side by side on the little bench in the packed room, and an elderly man got up and asked Mooji a question. It was the first of a handful of dialogues that afternoon. As Mooji responded, I noticed that David was very attentive – he seemed moved. Afterwards, he was quiet, thoughtful, and later he told me what had touched him.

'I can't put my finger on it. I remember Mooji talking about what a huge effort it is just to be a person, to keep up the persona, and something clicked,' he said.

The old man said that people sometimes ignored him and that he often felt a sense of rejection: a lack of regard or respect from others. This had affected his whole life, he explained, and he lived behind a protective screen that prevented real contact with people, including himself. He could no longer stand it, but he was stuck, unable to drop the façade and incapable of freeing himself from this pattern, which always led to disappointment and sadness. How could he let go?

In response, Mooji talked about identity and the ego: 'When we believe ourselves to be a person, which is not a real *thing* but a constructed identity – the result of conditioning, projections, thoughts, fears, memories – we suffer. The *true self* is actually at peace, always. It doesn't need recognition from others – it doesn't need anything. It is not *self-important*. It places no importance on the constructed self: the façade.'

'Self consciousness and self-importance – they're the same thing. Whether we think ourselves to be very grand or very small, we are playing the same game, and my focussing on how I am *seen* is all about self-importance,' David said. 'I've always tried to do things properly, to appear capable and in control of things and not to look a fool. I hadn't really thought it through; it was all unconscious. I could never do well enough – never be satisfied. Why couldn't I just relax and be *real*, even if real meant fallible, human, even ridiculous?' he said. 'What if I just drop it? What if it really doesn't matter how I am seen? It's so obvious, but until you see it, really *see* it...'

It was as though David had shown up on exactly the right day; the day when someone exposed something that he recognised was relevant to his own story, something simple yet profound that resonated strongly with him and had been hidden until then. Whilst I had undergone a slow and gradual change of perspective, David had suddenly woken up to this realisation and its implications. Now, it seemed, we were on the same page at the same moment.

Something had led me to make this journey, and it must have brought David here too. I was filled with gratitude for having arrived at this place, seen and heard Mooji and visited this extraordinary community. I felt very warm, loving and close to David, and after so much doubt it now seemed obvious that our relationship was exactly the right compost for us at this point in our lives. It could support us and we could help one another to remember who we are, and what we are not. It all made perfect sense.

Part Three

Part Three

Today I am sitting alone on my bed, which I haven't done for some time. I am staying at a campsite at the eastern end of the Algarve's built-up tourist strip. It's spacious, homely, laid-back and only a short walk from the sea. Like the one in Sagres, it's sited alongside a patch of rough land, which is home to a collection of farmyard animals and poultry, along with feral cats, donkeys and dogs. I guess it's not everybody's cup of tea, but I have come to love staying next to these noisy creatures as they mingle together in their happy little communities. I like being so close to their world. The air is filled with sound. I hear cockerels and goat bells, a goose or two, the twittering of small birds and flies buzzing around my head. None of this bothers me. A dog now joins in with the cacophony. Through the window I can see sparrows pecking the ground where I shake out my breadcrumbs.

I have no plans for now, except to be here, walk on the beach and see what happens. From here it's only an hour's drive to the border with Spain, which I plan to cross in a couple of weeks. Until then, I am enjoying being settled and cramming in as much idleness as possible before I leave Portugal. Sun pours in through the rear windows and I am basking in its warmth like a lazy cat. I have no urge to move.

I remember something I had almost forgotten: back in October, the psychic had said, 'After that...' He told me that it was not something to fear, just my grandfather's message. I had a feeling it was significant, but after *what?* And *what* after that? I let it go, trusting that all will reveal itself.

*

David left a few days ago. After visiting Mooji we spent two weeks travelling around the southwest of Portugal, eating, drinking and being very happy and harmonious. We walked, chatted with fellow travellers, swam, combed beaches, made driftwood sculptures and relaxed into simply being together.

One of the things we love to do is visit ancient Celtic sites and look at megaliths. We have seen some fantastic menhirs in Brittany – some thirty feet tall – and the amazing system of three thousand standing stones at Carnac. I can really imagine myself becoming a bit of a megalith anorak. One day, driving away from a small village where we had stopped for coffee, we were thrilled to spot a sign saying 'Megaliths 5 km' and decided to take a look. I had heard that there were some amazing ancient Celtic sites in Portugal and had a vague recollection of a site in Alentejo that was one of the most significant groups of menhirs in the whole of Europe. What a stroke of luck it was to find ourselves chancing upon something as exciting as this! We turned onto a small lane and seemed to drive for miles before we saw a second sign. Here we turned onto a dirt track that lead to a bridge which had been severely flood-damaged, but we decided to push on.

Getting across what remained of the bridge was a challenge. We had to drive carefully over broken slabs of concrete which had collapsed into the shallow river, but we were determined to see the spectacle, having come this far, and we made it across. The track was rough and winding and took us far out into the wilds, among gently undulating meadowland and stunted, lichen-covered trees. Just as we were wondering if we had gone wrong, we arrived at the end of the track in a small parking area, and looked around for a path to the site. But there was no path, and there were no further instructions. We stood there casting about and then noticed something among the low trees. There, surrounded by a metal fence with a small information board, were two stones, each about the size of an adult sheep. We had a good look, giving them as much reverence as we could muster, before getting back in the van, muttering about how size isn't everything, and returning along the bumpy track, back across the broken bridge and onto the long, winding lane to the main road.

David had been profoundly affected by the visit to Mooji and told me he felt permanently changed by the realisation that came to him. He was more happy and relaxed than I had ever known him to be – more at home in himself. He had simply dropped the exhausting effort of trying to be someone, trying to keep up the identity of a person who always gets things right. He had realised that there was no fear involved in this. Indeed, what he had let go of was fear itself: fear of ridicule, fear of being inadequate, fear of feeling small – the fear that his thoughts had taunted him with, and in which he had believed. Like ivy on a tree, fear had grown around him and attached itself to him, but was *not* him.

Now we were entering a new place: a new mode. The world seemed bright, fresh, and strangely amusing. We laughed a lot, not about anything in particular; everything just struck us as funny. Life seemed enchanted – whatever was happening. It was beautiful to watch David soften and open up. I had thought our time together might have come to an end, and now I saw that it had not; not yet, maybe never, maybe any minute.

*

It was my dad's birthday, so I phoned him to wish him many happy returns of the day. He was pleased and told me he was proud to have such a brave daughter. This is something he has expressed a few times lately in his occasional emails, and I notice that it doesn't land well with me. In fact, I feel frustration rising each time, even though he is paying me a compliment. At first I thought this was because I felt fraudulent. After all, I was having what might be considered a very long holiday, not doing humanitarian work or serving as a soldier. I wasn't really sure what my dad thought I was doing.

I sat quietly and tried to see what was hiding in the shadows. I found myself back at the same point: my darkest time. My dad has an adventurous spirit and a great deal of courage, and he admires these qualities, which I guess he saw manifesting in me when I took off on my single-handed adventure. All my life, I have had conflicting feelings around my relationship with my father – as do many daughters, not to mention sons. We were so inevitably and closely entwined, yet we came from entirely different worlds. I have never been able to fully appreciate the passion for adventure that drives people to achieve seemingly unnecessary feats. I was concerned with other areas of life, content merely to survive, to stay afloat emotionally and, hopefully, to create a stable family environment for my children. Competitive sport, adventure and ambition were outside of my field of understanding and beyond my capability.

Courage, however, is something I do understand, and I had been brave too, in an area that my dad might not easily recognise. I had faced and survived the disintegration of myself: a serious mental health event. At the time, I told him that I was unwell and couldn't work, but I'm not sure if he could translate what I was telling him. His experience hadn't given him anything he could use to understand or help me. I guess he could not cope with the idea that one of his children was suffering from a mental condition, steeped, as these things have always been, in stigma and shame. Perhaps it was easier for him to shut his mind to the possibility and ignore me until I pulled myself together. At the time, I felt angry and disappointed. I thought he didn't care. Going on an adventure, on the other hand, has no stigma attached to it. It is something positive. I was a success – he could recognise that.

I survived almost by myself. I am not trying to be heroic; it's just that it had to be that way. I now see that the only way I could reap meaning and reward from that experience was to go through it as an adult, alone and on my own terms, discovering what it really meant for me. To get rescued could have meant having my experience interpreted into something else, something that jarred with labels like 'normal' or 'healthy'. I might have been *cured* of my *illness* and the process could have been cut short, forced back inside. My episode sprang from an unbearable dissatisfaction deep within me. The discomfort pushed me into a radical process of change. It was traumatic. It appeared that I was losing the plot – not a good look to the untrained eye.

Was that really illness, or can it be viewed differently? Not everyone survives such a breakdown. I think of my friend who took her own life, the one who I felt to be present after the clairvoyant meeting. Of those who do recover, some come back and rejoin life as they knew it. Others find themselves in a new place, viewing reality from a fresh perspective. I wonder if the ones who didn't survive might have had more of a chance of recovery if their experience had been defined differently, and if they'd had support to help them walk through the fire.

In the event, out of absolute necessity, I found a well of strength and resource from deep within myself – even beyond myself. I dredged up all the courage and faith I could find there. I had to be still and trust that grace would bring me through.

Back then, I didn't understand my dad and he didn't understand me, and I made the assumption that this lack of understanding equated to a lack of love. At the time, that was another huge blow, which added to my feelings of distress. There was a war going on inside me. There was the love I had for my father versus the judgements I made about him. There was the love he had for me versus his actions and values. I now know that this equation was inaccurate. Despite miscommunication, differing world views, disappointment and other things that have periodically entered the frame over our lifetime together, beneath them all has been indestructible love. It is only now, as I look from this new place, that I can see that the love is undiminished. Love is the constant force that lived and lives, survived and survives, and finally surpasses all the other factors. Love is the only important thing – the only real thing. The rest is a bundle of thoughts about how it should have been. 'Should' is a dangerous word.

*

It is fascinating and fulfilling, this process of dissolving, of realising what I am not, what I am and what is simply *happening*. I guess I am trying to stay with the Truth and not to get distracted by thoughts, which, when I really look at them, seem to be random chatter about all sorts of things. My mind leaps from the past to the future, to worries, then to judgements about what I see and hear. One thought leads to another, often along vaguely logical lines, but it all seems fruitless. How much truth is contained in the running commentary of my mind? It's frequently irritating and sometimes stressful. The Truth is, for me, the space that remains when all that chatter loses its grip. Truth is not opinion or belief, a concept or an idea: it is a state, and when I experience it, I see it – I know it. I don't need further proof.

Growing up, I never wanted to immerse myself in news coverage or the stories of misery told by people around me, including teachers and other adults; yet I was all but commanded to listen. It felt like my duty – proof that I was good and caring. It was deemed a sign of intelligence, and there seemed to be a degree of nobility in suffering alongside fellow humans across the world who were experiencing horrendous things. I noticed that if I subjected myself to a daily bombardment of terror and misery, I became terrorised and miserable. And then what could I do to change anything, or to help?

Now, to an extent, I am off the hook. I am relatively free because I refuse to subject myself to repeated doses of distress. But does that mean I don't care? Surprisingly, I am not out of touch. In fact, the less I am swamped by the horrors of the world, the more I feel connected to all life. I share the pain; I grieve; I cry. My mind tries to make sense, make judgements, and I see that it can hijack the situation, afraid of the powerlessness of not knowing what to do about atrocity and injustice. Can I save anyone? Can I change anything? What if I can't? What if I can only love?

Trying to save the world from suffering would be like trying to empty the sea, possibly using a sieve. To end my own suffering would be a start. But that doesn't mean changing outside circumstances, nor expunging myself of feeling. If I can stay quiet for a moment and stand apart from the mind's commentary, I find that it is in the heart that we are all connected. The quality that I bring to the world when I am in a state of fear and suffering is not helpful to anyone or anything. A change in my own state of consciousness could be my greatest contribution to saving the world from suffering. It might seem small, and it might sound selfish, but it feels truthful to me. And it might be the best I can do.

For me, it seems, the first step is finding and cultivating peace – a space in which a sense of connection and empathy with all life naturally grows. From this compassion springs an impulse that feels positive, stable and genuine. It is a force that leads to actions which will not be thwarted by doubt or feelings of powerlessness.

*

My Swedish friends caught up with me here at the campsite next to the lovely, noisy animals. I spent some time with Ivan, as Maira was away for the week. He was good company; we went for walks and sometimes ate lunch together, sharing ideas and silence. Ivan challenged me with questions that were hard to answer. Perhaps this was because the questions were unanswerable – more Zen *koans* – and they invited a simple experience of truth rather than a lot of mental gymnastics. Ivan has been a great teacher, and when I told him that, he replied that I was a teacher for him, too. Everyone we meet is a teacher, it seems, in one way or another. I enjoyed our discussions and the sense of space and peace I experienced. I felt that, yet again, life had given me exactly what I needed. The phrase 'I feel blessed' seems to be rather overused these days, but that is how I felt: blessed.

One morning, Ivan invited me to join him for lunch – but not just any lunch. He wanted us to have what he called a 'present moment lunch'. The idea was that we'd walk along the beach to a seafront cafe, eat something delicious and return back alone the shore without uttering a single word that had to do with the past or the future. It sounded simple enough, and I agreed to go.

Off we went down the lane and along the the sand, as the sea sparkled and the clouds formed and reformed lazily against the deep blue sky.

'It's warm,' Ivan said, breaking our long silence.

'Yes,' I agreed.

'Nice clouds.'

'Hmm.'

'I'm quite hungry.'

'Me too.'

There was nothing more to say. I liked this game. As we progressed along the edge of the sea, I didn't even feel the need to comment out loud on the beauty of the scene. The mental chatter subsided and my mind emptied. Things just were. Walking and looking was more than enough. We arrived at the cafe.

'This reminds me of... Oops!' Ivan said. I laughed. The waitress arrived and we shared a bit of light-hearted banter with her while we ordered.

'Once I was in a restaurant...Ah! I've gone to the past!' I said. Ivan smiled.

We ate, we drank and we barely spoke. The silence was comfortable, enjoyable. It didn't feel awkward, because we had agreed to take part in an exercise together. It struck me that a lot of conversation consists of appraisal of current circumstance, memories and speculation. There's nothing wrong with any of it – it is through sharing stories of one sort or another that we connect – but sometimes we are just filling the space out of habit. The purpose of the present moment lunch experiment was to become aware of the mind and the way it operates, continually skipping through the data bank searching for relevant or even random snippets. It's an exercise I had never done deliberately before, yet it felt familiar. It reminded me of being alone as a small child, rock pooling for hours. There must have been a time when I lost the ability to spend time deeply absorbed, complete and joyful like that. As an adult, swimming and pretend-surfing give glimpses of that same magical sense of being totally at one with the moment, present in the present.

I loved our silent lunch and I decided to use the idea again whenever I notice my mind goes off on one of its spins. And there I was again, projecting into the future.

*

It's the coldest night yet and I am making tea at four in the morning, just to keep warm. Myfanwy is great as a runner and as a camper, but for a long trip that includes nights spent under clear winter skies, I probably need a better insulated van. Since the rain stopped, the atmosphere has been very dry: perfect for airing the bedding. Writing has been difficult, but my days are blissful, idle, warm and restful. My old sleeping pattern has returned, but I am very relaxed about it now. I notice a strange background noise. It must be the sea half a mile away; why is it roaring when there's no wind? Why is it crashing when there are no waves?

Just before David left, something happened. It was as though a magic spell had been cast. In our last two weeks together we seemed to have found harmony and joy. It was a little surprising at first. Our final moment together in the airport felt like a frame from a slightly cheesy, romantic film. As he was about to board his plane, we just stood and stared at each other. Our edges had vanished – they sort of dissolved and for a moment we merged into one, everything else had disappeared. It was as though our hearts had opened and swallowed us up.

Since then I've not felt alone or separate. I feel complete and I enjoy him thoroughly, even without his physical presence. I love the fact that we've had such a journey together and I love having space for myself too. He told me on the phone that he feels transformed. I think we have both fallen in love! Love is the most wondrous thing to be in. This is not personal love, though. It's as if we have fallen into Love itself – into our hearts.

*

It's said that if you think you are enlightened, you should try spending a weekend with your family. Spending several months away from all things familiar has proved to be an opportunity to see everything differently. I don't know about the mind, but travel does seem to broaden the vision. I was feeling frustrated, bored and stale before I left home. The stagnant life can be a breeding ground for all sorts of things – complacency, for example, and indeed contempt. I had a kind of road rage response to being stuck. I just wanted freedom. Freedom meant movement, motion, going. And then freedom came to mean stillness.

Even so, Saturday evenings can often feel tricky for me. There's some old wiring at work that makes me expect to be at a party or some other social function on a Saturday night. Now the days are short, and today has been cold, wet and increasingly windy. This long Saturday evening has been a little lonely. I was expecting a call from David, but he didn't phone. I had that annoying expectation/disappointment equation going on.

Yesterday I spent the whole day in silence, which I loved – in fact, I felt I could have spent all week in silence. Tonight, though, I have thoughts nagging at me, and I can't make them stop – it comes and goes, the monkey mind. Where's my mindfulness when I really need it? I am trying to use this discontent as grist to the mill: my challenge is to observe my silly thoughts, to try to watch and not get involved. Then I try to try without trying, which is tiring, so I stop trying anything and get into bed. Myfanwy is getting buffeted in the gale and it's like being on a boat. I am cosy under my duvet, listening to the wind and the rain battering the van. Underneath it all, I am all right.

The storm has passed. Dark clouds move swiftly across the sky, which is surprisingly bright this morning. This reflects how I feel: there's something steady and calm holding the clouds. There's a sinking feeling in my body, but *I* am not sinking, not really. I finished reading a novel last night. The ending was never going to be happy; the protagonist drives off a cliff to his death. It was only a story, and, thank God, it's not *my* story.

My own drama started where the book left off: David finally phoned, long after I had given up on him for the night. He was standing – swaying, I imagine – on a windy cliff, having enjoyed a large number of drinks at a party. That was a rather alarming image. He told me more about the cliff: it was the place where we had taken a walk among the crags and flowers last May, after which we had visited friends for a quick drink, when I was despondent about our impending homelessness and David drank too much and snapped.

Last night brought the whole episode right back into focus. Why was this horrible memory coming up now, just when we had found real harmony? Was I being tested somehow? Could I handle those difficult feelings now that I believed I had learned to love my own company and let go of so much old baggage? I decided that this was a golden opportunity to find out – I would simply go on with my day, trying to stay present and to trust that all is well.

I revisit Ivan's question: 'What would happen if you just accepted David exactly as he is?' I see once again that it's my judgements and ideas about how things should be that are making me uneasy. In fact, I am here doing what I am doing, and he is there, possibly at the bottom of the cliff, or perhaps just suffering a hangover. While there is behaviour that I choose not to put up with because it affects me directly, I also have to accept the things that are not my business. Relationships bring these into close proximity, and it can be hard to distinguish between one's own genuine needs and boundaries and the tendency to manage other people based on judgements about how they should conduct themselves. What would happen if I stopped the judgements and the 'shoulds'? Perhaps I would be relieved of the weight of inappropriate responsibility. It feels good to recognise this. The physical distance between us helps me to see this with greater clarity.

All that I can perceive around me is real: as real as it ever gets. Everything else is imagined, projected or remembered. When I stop concerning myself with what is possibly going on elsewhere, I no longer suffer. I find that all is well. I notice the uneasiness – I am watching it. The trick is to *stay* in this moment, right here, in this awareness – something we are not trained to do. My task now is to practise this way of seeing, and that is enough work for me. I try.

I remember something. On that dreadful May weekend, when I was so disappointed, hurt and shocked, I longed to leave immediately. I wanted to get into a car and drive until I was far away. I didn't know Portugal then, but I craved the distance and unfamiliarity it offered. Now the memory is revisiting me – or am I revisiting the memory? Anyway, here I am in Portugal. I am right *here*, in the place I longed to be. I try to focus on the cockerel crowing. My mind sneers: 'How long can you keep that up? You can't always stay in the present moment!' That's the mind: obsessed with time, projecting into the future, regurgitating the past. I guess I can listen to the cockerel as long as he is crowing, and the birds are singing now, too.

*

I spoke to David again this afternoon and he was fine; there had been no disaster. He too had revisited the bank holiday incident, which he found painful and shocking. It had been a wake-up call at the time, he said, and he felt that the person who behaved so destructively that night was long gone. There is no going back. We have moved on. Could it be that we have both come to terms with the fact that, for us, there is no ideal home with a beautiful little garden, but that something else has come our way?

*

The eastern Algarve is quite lovely. I am free camping near the fishing village of Santa Lucia for a few nights, waking to a beautiful, ever-changing view of salt marshes and creeks, sharing this delightful spot with friendly campervanners who, like me, are in love with Portugal. I ride my bicycle along the coast road each day in the warm sunshine under a deep blue December sky. I walk along the promenade lined with palm trees and look out at the blue, green and white fishing boats tied up along the shore. I feel very much at home here, chatting to cafe staff, drinking coffee at outdoor tables and watching life happen around me.

I swam in the sea yesterday, which was wonderful. The days are short and the nights are cold. I feel like a mermaid in my sleeping bag. It's one of those shaped like a coffin, so my feet are close together, zipped in tight; my upper body is free under the huge duvet; my salty, sandy hair falls round the pillow. I am slipping under the surface, sinking into the darkness, into the depths of dreamland.

*

I notice that I find it so hard to make decisions. Shall I stay in this place or move on? It doesn't seem to get any easier, and perhaps this is because it really doesn't matter where I am.

Still, I find myself getting a bit restless and lonely these days, just for moments. This is a new thing and I wonder if I have simply done what I came to do. Maybe I cannot go any further at this time. I don't want to backtrack either – I must keep moving, however slowly, towards home.

There comes a point when the traveller has reached the furthest extremity of a journey – the point at which she turns the nose of the horse in the direction of home. The feeling changes: suddenly there's no longer the anticipation of what lies beyond. Even though the return trip might take a different route, the sense of curiosity and mystery that was present on the outward journey subsides. It's a psychological shift, like the difference between breathing in and breathing out. And the out-breath is almost a sigh of resignation or relief. However, I still have a long way to go. Christmas, New Year and the journey back to Wales are all things that I will have to live through. Why am I thinking ahead and feeling as though I have run out of steam?

*

It's time to say farewell and start a journey that I am not sure I want to make. After three months in Portugal, I am about to head for Spain to meet up with my son, who, along with his little family and some friends I have never met, has rented a house in the mountains above Malaga for Christmas. At eight thirty this morning, a huge JCB came and started noisily digging up the ground right next to my van. It was clearly a sign to get moving.

I enjoyed a final coffee in a tiny coastal village en route, one of the few places where the old Algarve can still be seen. There were fishing boats, small houses and a beachside shack that served as a cafe, perched beautifully where the thickly wooded landscape ends and the rocky, sandy shoreline begins. All too soon I was crossing the Guadiana river, the border, this time with a deep sadness. Immediately the views were different. I had left a softly undulating green landscape, and now I saw only a hard road bordered by endless parched vegetation.

I drove for hours, with a sinking heart and an ambivalence about what I was doing. After all, I could have stayed longer in Portugal, driving slowly north through the areas I hadn't yet seen. But how could I pass up the opportunity to spend Christmas with my son when, by coincidence, he would be staying relatively so close? I longed to see him and I knew that, whichever way I travelled, the journey back to Wales would be long and I would be alone, something that had not been a problem until now.

Spain feels like a foreign land where I know nobody and don't understand the roads or the ropes. This is ridiculous, because Portugal was just as foreign to me when I first arrived there. Is Spain really such a different world or has something happened inside me? It's slightly disconcerting and I simply have to keep on going, snaking ever closer to Malaga.

I break the journey at a campsite, near an Andalucian town that's famous for the million pilgrims on horseback that gather here every year, but today the whole scene is almost deserted. There are impressive churches and scores of hotels and bars, but its many wide streets are sand-covered and have the appearance of the set for a cowboy film. Outside each building there are wooden rails for tethering the animals. It's strange and fascinating, but I am not really in the mood for more than minimal engagement with this extraordinary place. I am in travelling mode and I just want to get to my destination, where

I imagine I will be able to relax for a week with my son and his companions.

The next day, having driven for hours up to and via Seville, of which I saw only the industrial outskirts and road systems, I arrive in a small town near Malaga, where I am hugely relieved to find the car park where I have arranged to meet them and delighted to be hugging my son. He warns me that the narrow mountain track to the house is in a poor state and will be a challenge for Myfanwy and me, so he will lead the way along the four miles of rough road. He has asked the owner of the rental house if she thought I could manage the track in an old, long wheelbase van. She replied that the track is certainly a challenge, but one that I should take. 'Just tell her to be patient and brave,' was her advice.

My son and his six companions were crammed into a seven-seater rental car with no room for their luggage, which had to be strapped to the roof. I followed them carefully along the bumpy, potholed track – so far so good. There was a place where the road had been washed away – a broad, deep ditch, now cutting right across our alarmingly narrow path – and continuing looked highly improbable; but somehow, by copying my son's precise manoeuvres, I made it across the divide. After that, I felt somewhat relieved, and relaxed into the dead slow pace as we bumped along, avoiding huge potholes and small landslips to one side and the edge of the dirt lane to the other. I was glad I wasn't driving one of those large, swanky Winnebagoes of which I have seen so many on my travels. Then the climb began. Up and up we went, and I began to feel nervous as the land dropped away sharply just beyond the rim of my tyres. I hoped that nothing would come the other way.

Progress was slow and the road got steeper. Now there were

hairpin bends to negotiate, and I had to keep my speed up to manage them successfully. My heart started thumping and I knew that all I could do was keep going. I hadn't thought it would be *so* steep and *so* bendy. We were now snaking around the edge of a mountain. This section of the track had been nicely concreted – which must have been a tricky job – but it was very close to the precipice, from which we were protected only by a low metal barrier, good lane control and grace. Up ahead I saw the rental car disappear, putting on a bit of speed in order to get up and round the final set of hairpins. I was horrified! Could we really make it?

The van is old, heavy and long, but there could be no going back, and I could not even consider stopping as I knew that Myfanwy's handbrake would not hold us. I put my foot down, steered like a demon and prayed. Three or four ridiculously sharp and steep bends, a rising cloud of dust and gravel, and we made it! It was the most terrifying drive of my life. I sat shaking and sweating and almost in tears. Getting out of the van, I made it absolutely clear that I would never, ever do that drive again. Now we could settle in for a week of festivities – a week in which I would have plenty of time to contemplate driving back down that infernal helter skelter. There was no alternative.

*

The sky is huge and bright blue. We are high up in the sierra, perched at the top of a mountain, looking out over a system of peaks which are speckled with dark bushes and look surprisingly green for this parched region of Spain. Silvery grey gravel tracks appear and disappear as they weave their way among the contours and lead to white houses dotted about on the mountainsides, some almost at the top of the pointed peaks. Small trees cling to the more sheltered of the slopes. I have to admit it is spectacular, even though there is a part of me that has already decided I don't like this place – the part that is engulfed in fear. Can I bring myself back to the present moment and enjoy all this beauty? Standing on the veranda, I can just see the coast in the light, distant haze beyond the dimishing mountains. I guess that this is part of the reason for building villas in such unlikely looking locations: that view and the remoteness, the peace. Our accommodation is a wooden cabin with a tiny terrace upon which stands a small pool. The water is freezing cold.

We sit around the kitchen table eating and drinking, and I start to get to know my new companions: the family who are sharing this week with my son, his girlfriend, Lara, and her adorable son – technically my step-grandson – Mica. Baz and Kerry are old friends of Lara and they have two teenage daughters, who are hiding out in their bedroom in the loft. Kerry takes sandwiches up to them. I sleep on a mattress on the sitting room floor – not as comfortable as my sofa bed in Myfanwy.

Next day, there's a shopping trip and a visit to the beach. I haven't recovered from yesterday's ascent and I decide to stay at the cabin. Mica wants to hang out with me, so when the others all go off, the two of us take a walk further along the ridge. We follow the track up and down and round and round, passing the occasional villa, listening to the silence. Sometimes Mica hums to himself. He has his arm around my waist and mine is round his shoulder. The morning sun warms our backs as we try to step on the single gangly shadow we throw out in front of us.

Strolling back towards the cabin I can see the dreaded track, now far below us, with its absurd hairpins. These treacherous routes are the only access for vehicles carrying the materials needed to build all the dwellings up here in the sierra. How on earth do they manage? Looking down from here I can't believe Myfanwy made it. I feel slightly light-headed and focus on getting back to the cabin for coffee and cake. Eventually the others return with supplies, and we eat again at the large wooden table. The two girls are still too shy to join the party.

The next afternoon, my son says he feels ill and goes to bed. He has a raging temperature and a fever which makes him delirious. It gets worse: he is burning up one minute and shivering uncontrollably the next. I try to stay away from thoughts of doctors or a trip to A and E in Malaga, and especially the journey that would take us there. I lie on the big bed and cuddle him in a way I have not cuddled him for many years. I stay there all afternoon, putting cold flannels on his forehead while everyone else sits on the veranda. At one point, Lara pops in and says she thinks this is a great chance for us spend some mother/son time together alone: a rare treat. I am grateful for the opportunity, though I suspect she is rather pleased to be relieved of the job of mopping his brow, as bottles of cava are being popped open outside in the sunshine. Lara swept my son off his feet a couple of years ago, and I find their relationship unfathomable. She is a funny mixture of cool and warm and I haven't got the measure of her yet. Her dark and attractive appearance often prompts people to ask if she is Spanish or Brazilian, when actually she's Welsh.

My overheated son sleeps, then wakes, and we talk. In the

strange bubble of his sickness we slowly, quietly talk about our life together, from his birth to now – twenty-five years of shared memories.

'You do know how much I love you, don't you?' I say. I am not sure where this has come from. Perhaps it has to do with my thoughts about my dad on his birthday.

'I think so, if it's possible to know,' he says, half into the duvet.

'It's hard to live through life's ups and downs and always be a good mother. I didn't know how to be consistent, and I'm sorry. I hope you can forgive me.'

'I can't think of anything that requires forgiveness,' he says. This makes me cry.

'I know I have let you down at times, and you can tell me if I've been an idiot.'

'You've been an idiot,' he laughs, 'just like everyone else.' We both laugh, tears still rolling down my face. He sleeps again for a couple of hours, then wakes, saying he feels quite a bit better.

It's a few days before Christmas, but it doesn't feel like it. It's hot, dry and sunny. The two teenage girls come out of their lair and sit at the window, looking awkward. I pretend not to be too interested in them and casually offer them tea and a piece of cake. I make a stupid joke and see the hint of a smile on their two very similar faces. I can't fix their names to them yet. They are strangers, but I know I like them.

Someone finds a delicate bare branch and we make it into a Christmas tree, standing it up in the sitting room. The twin-like girls make little origami decorations from wrapping paper and Mica hangs them on the spindly tips of the tree. This activity breaks the ice; they show me how they fold the paper and start to talk about their interests. The older girl wants, more than anything, to go to Japan. The younger sister is stressed about exams and feels she should not be here in Spain, but ought to be at home studying. This seems sad to me and nothing like the way I approached my education when I was fifteen.

We cram into the car one day, – Mica on my lap, his head crooked awkwardly against the roof – and drive to Competa, which perches at six hundred metres above sea level. It is further up into the Axarquía, so we don't have to take the scary track back towards the coast, but this road through the sierra is not one I would want to negotiate in Myfanwy either. Anyway, she is having a much needed rest among the scrub near the cabin. Competa is a small, ancient town, famous for wine, and so we spend some time in a bodega, sipping from little glasses until we have tried them all. From medium sweet to extremely sweet, they are all delicious and fragrant, and of course we buy a few bottles to take home.

After that, we wander off in various directions, arranging to meet later. Soon I notice the younger of the girls walking alone. I catch her up and see that she is crying. As we walk and talk, we link arms, and within a short time we have become friends. I can really relate to how she feels: her bewilderment with life, her lack of comprehension when she and her mother have a row – as has just happened, it seems. She simply can't get it right, and yet I can't see what could have gone wrong. I think about the way I felt in Portugal when I couldn't be honest with Maira, how it took me right back to my young self and my fear that to be myself and express my needs would set me at odds with my mother. We form a bond that continues over the rest of the holiday. We talk freely and she smiles a lot. Now and then we wink at one another across the table. I wish I could help her, but I can't see how, apart from showing her how much I like her and listening to her. I can't get involved in what appears to be a long-running issue within the family.

I am conscious of the fact that I am a guest – someone's mum, piggybacking on a group holiday. I'm not sure if the deal has been negotiated between them all, or whether my son and his partner invited me along without further consultation; after all, it was their idea, initially, to spend Christmas here. Either way, I wonder if my presence feels like an intrusion to this other family, who don't really know me. My intention is to be helpful and self-sufficient – and we seem to get along overall. However, I am aware of lapsing into judgemental thinking – if only within the privacy of my own thoughts. I feel sad for the girls who seem to come in for a lot of criticism from their mother. I get the impression that, deep down, Kerry is a soft and sensitive person, whose life has been tough and whose protective armour is a little spiky. She can seem fierce, often chastising the younger girl. Her husband, Baz, is a likeable and soft-spoken man, and I find myself wishing he would stand up for his daughters. I know it's none of my business and that I am only seeing a snapshot of their life, but I can't help feeling tense around this disharmony. I am caught between wanting to stand up for the younger child, who seems very vulnerable, and remaining quiet, staying away from my mind and its judgements. It's a dilemma.

I remember another conversation I had with Maira. I'd mentioned that some people ask the question, 'How can I get rid of my judgemental mind, my ego?' She'd laughed heartily.

'You can never get rid of the ego; it's a lifelong companion.

And it's not necessary to try – in fact, it's a complete waste of energy. Just be aware of it. Accept that it is part of your experience as a human being. It has a purpose, you know,' she'd said. 'Don't leave home without it!'

I find that helpful. The ego is like a default programme that repeatedly starts up and runs by itself. It has a function, but I don't have to let it run my life. I don't have to give it power through rapt attention and belief that it knows best. Just being aware of this is liberating – sometimes I forget that. Amusingly, it seems to be the ego itself that wants to get rid of the ego, so that it can feel good about itself or even superior to others, whom it likes to see as less aware. That strikes me as funny – a cosmic joke.

*

On Christmas Eve, everyone wanted to go to the beach, and I opted to stay home and cook dinner. The rental car was overstuffed already, so it was a sensible and fairly inevitable decision. I spent several hours alone, doing things I really enjoy: cooking and listening to music with a bottle of local wine. It was an opportunity to revisit myself in a way I hadn't done for what seemed like ages, yet was, in fact, just a few days ago. It was a welcome return to solitude: a time simply to be. It struck me that wherever I am, and whatever is happening, I can find sanctuary by staying quiet and letting my mind relax its grip.

On Christmas Day, we all sat around in the sitting room and watched while Mica opened dozens of little presents that his mum had brought from home in a big suitcase, along with a large bag of Brussels sprouts (she wasn't sure if they sold sprouts in Spain.) My daughter had sent a present for me with her brother. It was a CD she had put together for the remainder of my road trip. I put it on and, hearing the first familiar bars of 'Lay Me Down' by Crosby, Stills and Nash, I burst into tears. I wept through the whole song. Everyone was lovely; Kerry said, 'It's good to cry. Maybe they are tears of joy.' My son smiled. He knows me.

And they *were* tears of joy, but more than that, they were tears of *hiraeth*. To say that *hiraeth* is Welsh for longing is not enough – it is hard to translate – but I believe I *feel* its meaning. The Portuguese have a similar word: *saudade*. Both have to do with longing and nostalgia, with a sense of incompleteness, yearning, and the desire for something that might not even exist and may never have existed. Yet we know it – *I* know it. How is that possible? *Hiraeth* is often associated with the notion of home or homeland, yet I feel it as something else now. I am not sure I can explain.

I didn't want to leave, yet I longed for something. I missed my beautiful daughter and David. I missed all my loved ones – I longed to feel *at home*. And the song… the lyrics speak of all that has happened: how I have opened myself up to life, let go and been carried along by the endless river, not able to bend things to my will – no longer wanting to, most of the time. I have laid something down; I am on my way *home*. My tears were the tears of all those things colliding: of being really alive and vulnerable and strong; of knowing that I can trust life; of the sadness and the joy which were almost indistinguishable from one another in this moment.

Christmas can be a challenge. Sometimes, for me, it feels like a trial, but the week went quite well. No one killed anyone, and harmony won the battle over bickering, family dynamics and occasional sadness. It was lovely to spend so much time with my son, and the company was convivial. I wondered what I might have been doing had I not decided to spend the festive season in Spain. It might have been a lonely time.

*

I have been present at over fifty Christmases. There were the first few that I can't remember, followed by about a dozen that were all comfortingly similar and very magical – filled with ritual. There were sixpences in homemade puddings that my dad set alight, people I loved being together for days on end, and a feeling of wondrous anticipation that is lost to me now.

Then there was a clutch of Christmases that were more tricky – attempted re-enactments of the real thing that were scaled down and lacking in authenticity, or so it seemed to my critical, teenage self – and highlighted the fact that our family unit had collapsed. I had gone behind the lines, seen behind the scenes and found the reality to be a load of tinsel and packaging. They just had to be endured for the sake of others.

After I became a parent in my mid-twenties, things took a turn for the better and Christmases became our own: Peter's and mine, for *our* children. They had meaning again, even if we were complicit in spinning myth and illusion and purchasing tinsel and packaging. We became like children ourselves as we suspended our cynicism so that we could create our own family magic. It meant something.

Even though Peter and I separated a lifetime ago, we nearly always spend Christmas together with our children, our partners and sometimes a friend or two who is short of a family. The meaning of Christmas is different now. Sometimes it can still feel like something that has to be survived, but we get through it with a new attitude – almost a new vigour. Life is ticking away, and perhaps we are all aware that to be able to get together is a precious thing. To be here at all and to be lifelong friends are both things we appreciate.

*

The night before the dreaded descent, I barely slept. I was worried about the drive, about where to go next and how to spend New Year's. There was a campsite that had been recommended for its welcoming and friendly atmosphere, so I decided that I would go there – assuming I survived the drive back down the crumbling, potholed terror-slide. This time my son sat in with me, and at one point he had to get out and guide me, inch by inch, round the worst of the hairpins so that I could avoid launching myself off the edge of the precipice. I wish never to relive that event.

It was Boxing Day and we all said goodbye at the foot of the mountain. More than anything I was relieved to be on terra firma, and whilst the goodbyes pulled at my heartstrings, I was also just glad to be out in the world again, released from the intensity of Christmas in an isolated mountain cabin with people and their stuff.

I drove the short distance to the campsite and went to check in, whereupon I was barred from entry. I couldn't believe it. The receptionist had a good look at my van through the window and a good look at me, her eyes scanning me from head to toe. She asked me if I was alone. Why? I could not fathom it. She told me that I needed to be a member of some organisation to camp there. Nothing on their website or in my campsite book had alerted me to this. There was a lot shrugging and no flexibility. Did they think I was an undesirable type? 'Happy Christmas to you too!' I muttered as I left.

I found another campsite nearby, which was full – more shrugging – and then a third which was all concrete, the pitches so tightly crammed that I could barely manoeuvre. When I finally got into the tiny space, I felt pretty desolate. However, this journey has trained me for such experiences, and at least I didn't have to scale the mountain track again. I got on with the job in hand. I showered, ate, slept and left. What a handsome specimen was the young man at reception, and what a shame he was clearly in a job so entirely unsuited to his surly, unhelpful manner. I had to get out of this place and this mindset.

*

The drive from Costa del Sol to Murcia is long and winding. I wrestle Jamie Cullum out of the CD player and insert my daughter's compilation. It cheers me along as I head east. I don't like what I see of coastal Andalucia: all polytunnels and devastation, ugly concrete and intensive tourism. Murcia is a different story. It's not like Portugal – nothing is quite like Portugal – but it is magnificent: the sierras are speckled with pines and olive trees and shine golden as they catch the winter sun. I have been told of a campsite near the sea and figure this will be a good place to gather myself before I turn northwards in a few weeks, and head for home. I wind my way down the long lane to a small bay nestled between the cliffs.

The welcome at the campsite reception is a relief, and though pitches are expensive, I decide to stay here for a while and regroup after what has been a slightly stressful period. Apparently, this campsite has a vibrant social and music scene. I haven't sung since I first arrived in Algarve, so that sounds very enticing. What better way to commune with people than to sing and play music together? I realise I am missing my friends and family back home in Wales. I miss David especially, and I realise I could just hightail it out of Spain and go home in a few days, but it seems like there's still something I have to do here. I want to retune to the peace I had before – the peace that I felt ebbing away as I left the places I loved, where I had felt so much at home. I don't mind admitting that I am feeling a bit feeble, and that the past week or so has been tough.

I decided to go for a special campsite deal, which gave me a considerable discount and included electric hook-up, which I needed to heat the van on cold winter nights. It also meant I had committed myself to staying there for the next three weeks. It was very hard to decide what to do, as I was finding it difficult to stay in touch with my intuition. Once I had fixed on staying there I could just let go and see what evolved.

*

The clouds are bright and golden over the sea beyond the steep, craggy cliffs. I watch them slowly change shape as I sit in my van, drinking tea. The weather back home is awful, apparently, and I want to soak up as much sun as possible over the next few weeks. I am landing, allowing my soul to catch up with my body. Being here is an opportunity to practice surrender, to be with *what is* and make the best of the sun and the beautiful surroundings. I realise that the difficult mountain drive in

Malaga, the unfriendly campsites and the following long journey have made me lose my nerve, and I just can't see how I am going to get home. I wish I could just wake up there. I decide to postpone all thoughts on this subject for now.

*

I have been here for a week. I soon came to realise that it's less of a campsite and more a sort of expat compound with a small field for camping, which is empty. Nearly all the people here are long-term residents; most own little *casitas* – small, square units with verandas, some with tiny gardens – and others have caravans. There are scores of Dutch, German and English people crammed tightly into adjoining plots. A few of them are single men; none are solo women. They are not unfriendly, but they seem rather closed. I met an English couple who were kind to me when I arrived and invited me to their home, but then went on to tell me about the problems they were having with some of the other residents – I wasn't sure I needed to know about this.

I am parked next to an enclave of English residents who are from military backgrounds, and the conversations they have are familiar. They complain that Britain has 'gone to the dogs', then get onto the subject of immigration. They seem a little bitter and negative about it all, even though they now live in sunny Spain. These are not my people, but they invite me to join them for a drink, which is sweet of them, and I accept.

There are lots of little cliques here: Dutch couples in little groups and English folks who stick together. Someone mentions that the Germans don't mix with anyone, even other Germans.

There's a handful of Scandinavians here, too, and they seem more open and amiable. Alas, there are no other campers like me, staying in vans or tents. I begin to wish I had made a different choice and gone off by myself – but where to? Anyway, I have spent my budget, so I will have to live with it.

A modest music scene does exist. There's a small group who rehearse together and put on little performances in the bar. I decide to go and listen, and when I arrive I am told they are expecting me to join in. It was kind of them to include me – so, though I am unprepared, I sit with them and try my best to read lyrics and sing harmonies. I had hoped we'd get together in a friendly and casual way to share a few songs, just for the joy of it, but I wasn't included again after that. Maybe my voice was a bit rusty. When it gets dark at about six, I close myself in for the night, as do many of the others here. There's the bar, of course, but my appetite for sitting alone and drinking fizzy Spanish beer is limited. I have some films to watch on my laptop and David phones me every night.

A very sweet Danish man called Earnie came and knocked on my door to invite me on a walk he is organising. He is one of those thin, fit Europeans who walks and cycles many miles a day. Once I had explained that I am not, and do not, we planned a modest walk for the next day, on which we were joined by Earnie's son, Timmy. It was interesting to see some of the surrounding mountainous countryside, and as we shared a picnic of bread, cheese and fruit, I felt as though I had made some friends.

Earnie invited me to his place, and so I ventured up the steep cliff where his *casita* is perched, and from where the view is truly spectacular. He likes a drink and is extremely generous with glasses of chilled wine. There was nothing for it but to sit there all afternoon, drinking in the view and the wine and enjoying intelligent conversation. Both Earnie and Tim are very lively conversationalists and speak perfect English, which is handy considering my grasp of Danish. Finally I have found people I feel comfortable with.

*

A new visitor has arrived: another Danish man called Andrias. He is roguishly handsome, wears a jaunty hat and smokes cigars continuously. I met him on the beach where we shared some enjoyable conversation. He is here for a few days, visiting his friend who lives here. He is travelling alone and, like me, he feels he doesn't fit in here and would quite like to leave. I think he finds the place rather strange: densely populated, yet not particularly welcoming. We both harbour fantasies of escaping the intensity of the place in favour of 'the real Spain'. In another story I could imagine the two of us absconding under the cover of darkness and finding a beachside hotel where we would eat delicious food and chat with locals, the sound of a Spanish guitar wafting soothingly in the background. But then what? Anyway, we got on famously and decided to hook up for dinner at his place later.

Serenaded by a slightly off-station radio alarm clock, we ate a selection of fried up bits and bobs that we both had in our cupboards, accompanied by lots of red wine. Andrias sat right up close to me on the sofa, his pungent cigar smoke fogging the air, and confirmed my guess that he was in his late sixties. He advised me on many aspects of my life, which was sweet, but completely unsolicited. Smiling meaningfully and speaking rather slowly, he said:

'You know, every man wants a much younger, pretty girl. We are all the same, men, it's in the blood.'

'Is that so?' I enquired. 'And, by the way, how old do you think I am?' He thought I was thirty-seven, maybe thirty-eight, which I found hilarious, as I am over fifty. Soon I decided I was rather tired and ready to go home. He kindly offered me the option of staying at his place for the night to save me the trouble of walking home. I pointed out that I had arrived by bicycle and that the journey had taken me about ninety seconds.

'Yes,' I assured him, 'I am sure I won't change my mind.'

*

A couple of days ago, Andrias left and I was glad, because he had started to get on my nerves. I wonder whether I just don't like people – though there are some that I like very much. I seem to have rather limited tolerance for certain types of interaction. I wonder if I should be concerned about this. Anyway, Andrias popped in one morning while I was still immersed in tea ceremony – admittedly, this was after eleven – and I was in a bit of a bad mood. He wanted to show me a part of the coast path that he had enjoyed walking, so I joined him after a few minutes. From the very first moment he treated me like an invalid or small toddler, instructing me and guiding each footstep as if we were climbing a dangerous rock face, perhaps with ropes. Several times I told him that I was fine and could manage perfectly well. His advice continued:

'Now put your right foot here, and then...'

'I have walked a lot of coast paths, you know, we have them in Wales,' I countered with a little laughter in my voice. He wasn't listening to me.

'Your left foot there...' he coached.

'STOP!' I yelled, 'stop telling me where to put my feet!' He stopped walking, stood stock still and looked hurt. I felt sorry, but I couldn't take one more instruction – after all, I am not a pretty young girl wearing stilettos, nor an ancient matron with bad knees! Poor old chivalrous Andrias! I am sure he meant well, but do I come across as someone who needs this degree of extreme care? Maybe he was a frustrated outdoor-pursuits instructor.

I spoke to David last night and told him how I was getting on, how I had run out of steam and felt apprehensive about travelling all the way back to Wales alone.

'That's funny,' he said, and went on to tell me that he had been thinking that it would be fun to fly over and drive home with me. I was flabbergasted and then overjoyed. I had to ask him several times if he really meant it, and if he was sure he could spare the time? He was sure and we arranged that I would pick him up at Murcia airport in two weeks' time. I can hardly wait to see him.

My days are spent walking, occasionally swimming in the cold, rough sea, and sitting on Earnie's veranda, sipping wine, playing Scrabble and chatting. It's far from taxing, and yet sometimes all I really want to do is collect David immediately and go home with him. Even so, I recognise that these last days of independence are precious. Though it's warm and sunny here, it's still winter time, and I feel like hibernating. My idleness has reached a new level. Mornings are extremely lazy: the sun doesn't make it over the cliffs till eleven, so there's no need to rush.

I find myself feeling sad a lot of the time. Apart from my Danish friends, there's nobody I want to hang out with. I am in a slightly frozen state that has to do with feeling I am in the wrong place. If it wasn't for Earnie and Tim I think I would be considering this three-week stay a bit of a disaster. This is absurd, because I am sure there are many people who would love to be here, enjoying the warmth of the winter sun. I would like to leave, but I know that though I am somewhat uncomfortable, I have to stay with this, not run away. Life has something to teach me here. All I have learned is now being put to the test. I have to surrender to this reality and just watch my feelings and thoughts arise and dissolve; then I will be truly walking the walk, not just talking the talk.

*

Where do we go when we sleep? Maybe nowhere. Perhaps we are already there when we're awake, but with the TV on. When we sleep, the TV – the mind – is off; the room is quiet. We merge back into the ocean. Each night I wake in the small hours, a time that affords me a sort of secret space which can be quite creative. I am half awake and in an altered state, which feels like an opportunity to restore or reboot. In this mode, I gather some treasures that might otherwise be lost in the unconscious voyage of an unbroken night's sleep.

Having said that, today I have woken from a long slumber. In the bright light of a fine January morning, I feel that I have spent time with a wise teacher. Maybe that is what happens in deep sleep, whether we remember it or not. This morning I emerge with a strong sense of compassion for my father, who is so proud of me, his only daughter, for going off alone. I am no longer uncomfortable about this – and he has a point. This journey required courage, especially for a fearful rabbit.

The truth is, I have often been a bit cowardly, and like the lion in *The Wizard of Oz* I needed to leave the arena in which my life normally plays out and put myself into an unfamiliar setting, where I would have to find my courage to look at things differently. My dad is right: I am a brave girl. Does he know more than I credit him for? What if, somehow, he knows exactly what I am doing here, what this journey is really about? That would explain why he thinks I am brave.

Ivan once said: 'Your father is your greatest teacher.' We had been talking about my particular father, not fathers in general. I was sure he was right, yet I was not sure what I was supposed to learn. Now I think I understand what it is that I am learning from my father, or, more precisely, from our interconnection. This is not a relationship from which I can easily walk away. I have to face up to things – examine the truth. I had thought it was my responsibility to confront him about what I perceived as his failures: to tell him the Truth as I saw it. How arrogant that now sounds! Thankfully, something stopped me from embarking on this confrontation, which I had dreaded and procrastinated about for a while. Now I am looking from a new perspective. Before it's too late, I want to show my dad my love for him: the love that got obscured over the years, when our paths diverged; the love that is naturally born of our kinship; that I discovered is still there, despite everything.

*

The moon is full and bright and beautiful. I can't sleep. Writing has been hard lately and, despite my intentions to live in the present at all times, I am impatient to leave this place. It is like a small village with small village politics, where people are trapped together and petty squabbles are fairly common. Of the people who have talked to me, a lot either dislike the Brits, the Dutch, the Germans, or certain individuals. Strangely, though, they all seem united on one thing: this place is a paradise. I am happy for them, but I find it hard to love it here.

There seems to be a funny little argument that rumbles along. Some people love Spain and dislike Portugal, while other people I've met along the way take the opposite view. Maybe I, too, am indulging in this fruitless game of comparison. I can't help comparing my current experience with my time in Portugal, which seems a softer, sweeter, kinder country. Spain is vast and I hope I will get the opportunity to explore other parts of it one day, and maybe find more fondness for it. For now, though, I find myself missing the place where I felt at home.

I know that I cannot stop my mind performing its routine of grumbling, judging, comparing, nor do I need to – it's a waste of energy to try. All I can do is watch it happening, and as I do this, the thoughts lose their power over me. Just as I notice a thought, it changes shape, dissolves. I look back to that day when I sat in the morning sun at the campsite in France, at the very start of my journey. I remember writing about the endlessly chattering critical voice in my head. I recall how I wanted to be free from judgements. In the past I have berated myself for being too negative, too critical, not sufficiently Zen about everything. What has changed is that I now see the critical voice as distinct from me. I can listen to it, ignore, endure or enjoy it, because I know I am *not* it. There are unhelpful, unloving thoughts and uncomfortable feelings, but they are temporary – passing, like clouds – and beneath them is *me*: unshakable, stable, reliable. I am cultivating a deeper stillness which is hard to describe; it's as if I have gone from the surface of myself to the inner core.

Yet without a critical faculty, what would it be like to write a journal? Without it there would be no contrast, no dynamic and no journey. I see that my critical faculty is something I can use to look at life, rather than an impediment that defines me and causes me to feel discontent, or even shame. It's about using the facility of the mind rather than being hostage to it. I have skills, like discernment, that I can use whilst remaining rooted in an acceptance of how things are at any given moment. There's no conflict.

*

I am invited to dinner at the palatial caravan and awning of my neighbours, the English couple who have formed a little haven with other Brits. It's really kind of them to include me, whether or not it is just to make up the numbers, and I go along with an open heart and a bottle of cava. There are eight of us altogether: three couples, a widower and me. The food is tasty and the discussion lively. During the second half of the evening there is much agreement on the issue of immigration in the UK, our homeland, which, I am again told, has 'gone to the dogs.' I don't have much to say, but I decide to stand up for the plight of displaced people and families fleeing from war and persecution.

I suggest, as I did months ago to the dour Dutchman, that in the shoes of these unfortunate, poor and largely innocent human beings, we might also choose to risk our lives and flee to what looks like a better place and a more viable future.

There is a heavy silence during which everyone stares at me as if I have just said that I am a big fan of acts of terrorism. Looking disappointed, they clear their throats or shake their heads, and move on to another topic. For the remainder of the evening, the conversation continues between the four men, who discuss the pros and cons of various military tanks. All of them have experience with this sort of weaponry, and some have favourite models: excellence in engineering vies for position with the best capacity to destroy things. I am very quiet during this debate, having nothing to contribute and realising just how far I have strayed from my comfort zone. The other women sit in silent attendance, occasionally raising their eyes to the tented ceiling as if to say, 'Oh, these boys and their toys!'

David is due to arrive in eleven days. Can I make it? I guess I have to. How strange it is to be wishing for the days to pass quickly in 'paradise'. I guess the whole planet was once a paradise. Perhaps it still is, but we don't say that, because paradise has to look or feel a certain way. It's a matter of perception, or preference. I am glad the residents here love it. The more joy and love they experience, the better for everyone. I suddenly realise that coming here has done a job for me: it has made me really keen to leave. I had to come here to want to go back home.

*

Last night, I had my recurring dream about trying to catch a train. I know it's a common one, but this time, it felt overwhelmingly powerful and real. First I had to clear my desk, a huge oak-lidded thing in a classroom, because it was the very last day of school – not just for the summer, but for ever. Why had I not known this? I had to pack up a lot of stuff and carry it to the station. When I got on the train, I realised I had to buy a ticket; so, taking two pounds and leaving all my belongings in the carriage, I ran to the ticket office. The price of the ticket was actually three pounds and seventy pence! How could I get to the train to get more coins and back to the ticket office in time to buy my ticket, before the train pulled away with my books and bags on board? I woke up feeling genuinely panicked about the train leaving without me.

I realised that every time I have this dream, which has happened many, many times, it's always a train taking me home – never to some outing or adventure. Perhaps that's why it feels so frustrating: I just need to get back home. After this particular incarnation of the train dream, I thought: 'It's obvious! I am anxious about getting back to Wales.' Then it occurred to me that maybe the dream contained something deeper. It was the end of school: a major period of learning. My old life was finished, and I had learned all I could. It was about finding my way *home*: home to the safe haven that I had longed for, always. This is the sanctuary – the peace that I now know is my own being.

I think about *The Wizard Of Oz*. Dorothy wore the magic ruby slippers, so she had always had the means to get home, if only she had known how to use them. After she realises that 'there's no place like home,' she is shown how to click her heels together, which does the trick.

*

I might have run out of steam, but I have not run out of road. There's still a long way to travel, unless I want to take up permanent residence here. I am completely out of the habit of driving, but I get Myfanwy ready for the next part of my journey. I am finally leaving the strange community that has been my uncomfortable home for three exceptionally long weeks. Saying goodbye to Earnie and Timmy involved lots of hugging, and it was sad for all of us, I think. Myfanwy started first time and off we went up the winding road. For the first time in what seemed like months, I fed Tanya the coordinates of an official parkup for campervans. It looked very pleasant in my *aires* guidebook. I felt a tingle of excitement: I was back on the road. I loved planning a route and ending up at an *aire,* where I could stay for free (or very cheaply) and be anonymous. Perhaps I would take a look around the village on foot, find a bar, have a beer and feel free again.

After a while, we had negotiated the outskirts of a city and were tootling along a quiet country road, getting close to the place where we would stay for the night. Tanya announced that we had reached our destination. Only we hadn't. There was no *aire*, no sign; nothing but farmland. We explored the area several times in huge circles and tried different versions of the GPS coordinates, but it was no good. I pulled into a lay-by and just sat there. What was I going to do? I was definitely not going to drive back to 'paradise'. But where could I stay? I had to be at the airport first thing next morning to meet David. I wanted somewhere close by and totally safe. I have learned to use my instinct: if it feels safe, it probably is. But, more importantly, if I don't feel safe, I can't relax, and it only takes one scaremongering thought to queer the pitch. It would be foolish and somewhat arrogant to ignore what seasoned travellers and locals had told me about some areas of southern Spain being less than ideal for free campers, especially British ones. My gut feeling told me to be careful in this rural area, which I barely knew.

I sat for a while and then decided to ask for help. I had no choice but to trust in the invisible 'something' that I had almost forgotten about since my time in Portugal. I sat silently and felt the stress subside as I asked for guidance, vowing that if I got clear instructions I would follow faithfully. After a few minutes, the name of a place came into my mind very clearly, even though I didn't remember where I had heard it before, if indeed I had. I tapped it onto Tanya's screen and she showed me the route: not too far, somewhere east of the airport. I didn't have a mental picture of where I was, and all I could do now was follow Tanya's spoken instructions. I knew I could not let my mind come in and divert me from the blind faith I had promised as my end of the deal.

Eventually, we arrived at the small town with its unfamiliar name and drove along the narrow seaside road. We turned a corner, continued along, and then, to my great delight, I saw half a dozen campervans parked alongside some grassland. This was all I had hoped for: a group of travellers like me staying somewhere quiet, pretty and safe. There's something wonderful about free camping with other vans – it feels like home, like we belong there. We are just people sharing a space for a night or two, and, wherever we come from, whatever nationality, we share a love of freedom and nature, a respect for each other and a sense of equality and comradeship. Tucked between two large vans, I felt protected – part of a community.

The place looked to be the dream of some ambitious developer who had run out of cash; there was a strange juxtaposition of upmarket, newly built houses and empty, unfinished roads. It was hard to tell how many of the dwellings were inhabited, and there were hardly any people about. I walked around in the evening sun and felt very grateful. It was good to see the sea, and there was a beautiful sunset.

Next morning, I got to the airport early and waited for David's plane to land. I could hardly wait – he was the one person I really wanted to see. I did cry a little bit – it was such a relief to be reunited and to feel safe and supported when I had lost my nerve and, I guess, my joy. Very quickly and easily I found myself forgetting the tribulations of the previous weeks. We planned to spend a few days at my last free camping spot before making the journey to Santander to board our ferry in six days' time, with a couple of night stopovers. For a couple of days, we did the things we love to do when we are travelling: we walked along beaches, visited cafes where we chatted to the locals, played cards and Scrabble, talked and laughed.

We had heard of a campsite a few hours north that boasted a health-giving spa, fed by natural, mineral-rich hot springs. Floating about in a steaming outdoor pool sounded like just the sort of relaxing treat that would make up for cold January nights and having extremely limited access to bathroom facilities. We left the coast and wound our way up into the mountains at the northern edge of Murcia. David drove and I made the most of sitting back and taking in the ever-changing view.

This part of Spain is rich in natural beauty and cultural history, yet instead of exploring it, I had let fear get hold of me and lived, for three weeks, in a place I imagine is similar to any ex-pat compound, complete with high perimeter fence and a feeling of being somewhat isolated from the real world. Had

I simply got stuck? I would love to think this was my last dance with fear, but that might be wishful thinking. Fear is always sneaking in almost unnoticed. It takes my hand, gently at first, and we whirl around together, gathering pace. I lose myself, and by the time I notice, it has me firmly in its grip, paralysing me.

After everything I had learned about trusting life and living in the moment, I was still capable of letting my mind talk me into being cautious to the point of lunacy. The old programmes could still appear and start running my life. This was potentially disappointing. But the remedy was within my grasp. As soon as I noticed regret starting to goad me, I had a choice. I knew I could not waste another moment by berating myself for the time I had already wasted. Was it a waste anyway? Had I not learned or gained anything from my low patch? I had not run away. I had survived and handled it better than I might have in the past. Perhaps I had grown a little bit stronger.

We arrived at the spa and found a spot between two campervans. Most of the people here were elderly and German or Dutch. They all had plush vans in pristine condition and looked as though they had settled in for the whole winter. Every concrete plot was occupied, so we had been wise to book ahead. The weather was getting colder now, but the pool was pleasantly warm. One night at the site was enough for us, and the next morning we made an early start. Somewhere north of Madrid we pulled into a mountain village and found a small restaurant for a late lunch. There was a roaring fire, which was a relief as the day had turned bitterly cold; and as we were walking back to the van, snow began to fall. Before long we were driving through flurries of snowflakes, which were starting to settle on the road. The snow got steadily heavier and, suddenly, we had to slow down as we approached the back of a long queue of stationary lorries and cars on the gently inclining motorway, now thickly covered.

Snow ploughs were zooming along on the opposite carriageway, but on our side there was no sign of help, and all the lanes were blocked with vehicles. It didn't look good. Time spent at a standstill when you need to be moving toward a ferry port can seem to go very slowly. We consoled ourselves with the knowledge that, unlike some folks here, we had food and water on board, plus a loo and a bed. What was the worst that could happen? We surrendered to the fact that we might be here for a very long time, and then, suddenly, everything changed. A snow plough pushed past along the grass verge, and cars skidded about and set off in its wake. The lorries would have to wait for the next plough, and vans like ours spent a while trying to get a grip on the frozen slippery slope. I was impressed by the efficiency of the authorities in clearing the motorway, and I guessed that up there in the Picos they must be used to winter blizzards.

Once we were moving along again, we started to focus on the night ahead. We had found a campsite south of Burgos and fed its coordinates to Tanya. After that, all we had to do was drive and be guided to a place where we could hook up to the mains and get our heater on. The camping guide mentioned that the site was next to a wine cave, which was also something to look forward to. Maybe we could stock up some local wines to take home. As night fell, so did the temperature. We passed through the small town of Aranda and followed Tanya's familiar instructions. Leaving the main road far behind and weaving across the dark, deserted landscape, we arrived in a tiny hamlet of ancient, possibly abandoned dwellings, covered in thick snow and looking pretty in the beam of our headlights. This didn't seem like a place that would have a campsite open in January – and it wasn't. We'd been on a wild goose chase, on a cold, dark night, at the end of a long and arduous journey, and we began to feel slightly desperate. We just needed to eat and sleep. We retraced our tracks to Aranda and found a spot in an unromantic car park. After much-needed drinks and snacks in a bar we got into bed, fully clothed with all available blankets and a hot water bottle.

We woke to a clear sky and a hard frost, with a three-hour drive ahead of us, which seemed a doddle after the previous day's journey. However, our troubles were not over. After a while, we noticed that the sky up ahead had turned an ominous shade of charcoal. Once again we were driving straight into a blizzard. Just beyond Burgos, the police stopped us at a roundabout and directed us back into town, as the main road to the coast was impassable – and we resigned ourselves to the fact that we would not make our ferry.

We waited in a side street near the centre of Burgos for the snow to stop. It looked as though the bad weather had set in for the day, but it stopped snowing after a few hours. We drove through a mixture of snow and slush to the same roundabout, where the same policeman ushered us along in the tracks of the snow plough. It was quite a hairy journey, but we just kept on going, slowly but steadily, through another protracted snow storm; hardly speaking, but hoping and praying that we could make it in time for our crossing after all. As we descended the last twenty miles, the sky suddenly cleared and the sun shone brightly over the vivid green of the coastal plain. We wondered if the winter wonderland had been a dream, but, glancing back, we could see the snow-covered mountains and black sky.

We had planned to arrive in Santander with hours to spare so that we could go to a big supermarket and buy all sorts of goodies to take home, but instead we had to settle for a dash into a corner shop. Amazingly relieved that, despite all that waiting around in sub-zero temperatures, we had made it and got onto the ferry in time to sail back across the sea to England, we stood on the deck, looking over the railings, watching the coast of northern Spain as it seemed to slip out of reach. I felt something tug inside me. 'I'm going home after all my adventures. It's all over,' I said. David said nothing and squeezed my hand.

During the evening, in the ship's bar we met a man called Mark, who had spent many years travelling through Europe and North Africa. He now ran a business in Morocco and talked a lot about his experiences there. He also asked us about our travels, and I told him about some of my experiences. He laughed when we told him of our treacherous trip from Burgos: 'You came over the top in this weather? Are you crazy?' We – and Tanya, it seems – hadn't known about the nice, relatively flat motorway that went round the mountains. We had taken the most difficult route. Mark asked me what it was like to travel alone. I told him that I'd loved the solitude and also enjoyed meeting people, but that I was surprised I'd met so few solo female travellers along the way.

'Well, they're trouble, aren't they?' he said, in a matter-of-fact tone. 'Everyone gives them a wide berth 'cos they're not to be trusted. I've had nothing but hassle from lone women.'

It didn't feel as though he was levelling these claims at me personally, but it shed some light on something that had puzzled me on my journey.

'So do you really think people have a problem when they meet a single woman travelling in a van?' I asked.

'Yup, definitely. Couples shun them because they pose a threat to relationships, and single men wouldn't risk being taken for a ride of one sort or other.'

It had simply not occurred to me that I might have been viewed as this troublesome, threatening, desperate creature. I had never seen myself as anything other than a middle-aged woman wanting to learn self-reliance, see some beautiful places and find out who I was in the face of challenge and unfamiliarity. Mark's comments made me realise why I had felt so isolated in Spain, why I had been barred from the campsite on Boxing Day and why some people had treated me with caution: they'd probably been afraid that I was needy and might attach myself to them, or worse. Oh God! I had been so naive! And it was just as well; otherwise, I never would have set off in my humble, rusty little van, driving five thousand miles through strange lands. Also, I realised that, if what Mark said was true, I had been fortunate to have met so many people who did talk to me and treated me simply as a fellow traveller. Ignorance was bliss indeed.

Epilogue

It's halfway through the year and approximately midway between the end of my solo journey to Portugal and the beginning of my next trip. David and I plan to travel through France and northern Spain to Galicia, then meander down through the length of Portugal. There's so much that I want to explore in the north of the country, and we hope to be there when the almond trees are blossoming. I am very happy that we are going together and I think it will be a great adventure. I've come to love Myfanwy, and although I had planned to sell her after my trip, I can't part with her. She won't be coming on our next trip, though, as we are going in David's motorhome, which is a converted horse box. It will be slow, but it has all we need for a long winter voyage.

For now, though, I am here in west Wales, enjoying the summer and revisiting my adventure as I read the journal I wrote along the way. Writing about my trip has been an experience in itself, and yet, very much part of the journey. In fact, there has been no end. Since I returned home, my life has been a continuation of the process that started before I even set off. When I try to pinpoint the start, I can't find it. Was it the point at which I decided to go off alone? Or was it years before that, when it seemed that life wanted me to change, creating a storm and forcing me to find the still point in myself? Life is not explainable. I wonder if the Completion Backwards Principle has been operating by guiding my steps towards a destination that, all my life, I have always longed to get to: the discovery of my own state of peace.

The time I spent on the road was like time spent on an island, far away from all that was familiar and secure. It was a space into which something hidden became exposed and had the room to expand. It was not merely an escape, a temporary shelter; it was a an opportunity for revelation and transformation. The timing was perfect – I was ready. It took as long as it did for me to find home: home in myself. Now, it doesn't matter where I am: I am home. I remember my daughter taking a photo of me driving Myfanwy on the day we left Wales, and she posted it next to a picture of snails she found in a rock pool, with the caption: 'Other creatures who carry their home around with them.' That seems so apt, except that I discovered I carry my home inside myself.

Looking at my notes and remembering it all has given me another bite of the cherry. I am reliving it. Ultimately, the story had a 'happy ending,' though the last month was surprisingly challenging and felt like a test. I wondered if it would taint the entire thing, but it hasn't. Being on a road trip – really *being* – and being alone so much was extremely valuable, and I continue to benefit from it. It's not so much about the things that happened, which might later be remembered or forgotten, but more about a transformation – modest though it might seem – that took place. I gave something away, lost something that I have not been able, or inclined, to pick up again. I am changed. And while I see myself going through life's inevitable ups and downs, I know that I have met and made a life-long friend of someone I had never got to know very well before.

In fact, it is not a person. It is *me*: the being, the unchanging, the constant one who is there always, beneath the projections, the memories, the conditioning, the personalities that perform, the programmes that run. Beneath all that, before that, after that is something, or perhaps nothing. It is empty and yet full, completely satisfying and sufficient. Have I been brainwashed? I hope so! I hope my mind has been washed clean, and, to some degree, washed away. I do feel as though I have lost my mind, or, at least, I have been released from its grip. Things look different. Life is sweeter, softer and more joyful than I ever dreamed it could be.

I have come to see that to be alive, to consciously experience this incredible world, is precious beyond measure. It is miraculous. It feels like being madly in love. Life goes on with all its light and shadow, but inside there's a deeper, almost secret reality, one that everybody has, whether or not they know it. It makes me smile to know that the *real thing* is truly wondrous and it's always there underneath, just watching.